THE MARSHALL CAVENDISH
☆ ☆ ☆ ILLUSTRATED ☆ ☆ ☆
ENCYCLOPEDIA OF
WORLD WAR II

VOLUME 6

THE MARSHALL CAVENDISH
☆ ☆ ☆ ILLUSTRATED ☆ ☆ ☆
ENCYCLOPEDIA OF
WORLD WAR II

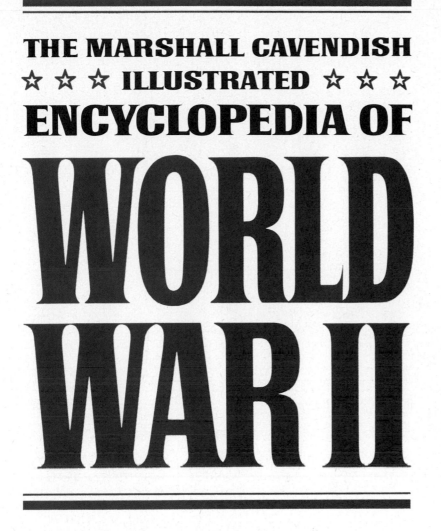

Based on the original text by
Lieutenant Colonel Eddy Bauer

CONSULTANT EDITOR

Brigadier General James L. Collins, Jr., U.S.A.
CHIEF OF MILITARY HISTORY, DEPARTMENT OF THE ARMY

MARSHALL CAVENDISH CORPORATION/NEW YORK

CONTENTS

Editorial Director: Brian Innes
Editor-in-chief; Brigadier Peter Young, D.S.O., M.C., M.A.
Managing Editor: Richard Humble
Editor: Christopher Chant
Art Editor: Jim Bridge

CHAPTER 52

Tobruk and Malta

Before zero hour on the desert front, the British and Australian Governments were involved in an incident with unfortunate consequences. Defeated in Parliament, Mr. Menzies' Liberal Government gave way to a Labour administration headed first by Mr. Fadden, then by Mr. Curtin. Australian opinion had become extremely sensitive following all kinds of alarmist rumours about Tobruk. Anxious to appease public feeling, the new cabinet demanded the immediate relief of the Australians in the garrison.

Whatever he said or did, the Prime Minister had to fall in with this demand, which was put forward in a most truculent manner, for however loyal the Dominions were to the United Kingdom, their relationship was between equals and decisions had to be negotiated, not imposed by Westminster.

Therefore, using periods of the new moon in September and October, a shuttle operation was organised, bringing into Tobruk General S. Kopanski's Polish 1st Carpathian Brigade and the British 70th Division, commanded by Major-General R. M. Scobie, and evacuating to Alexandria the 9th Australian Division and the 18th Australian Infantry Brigade

Group. In spite of the loss of the fast minelayer *Latona,* the operation was completely successful.

Nevertheless, Auchinleck's plans had been upset and, in spite of Churchill's irritation, he was obliged to postpone his attack from November 1 to November 18. Churchill could no doubt be criticised for his impulsiveness, but seen in the context of the overall situation, there was some rational justification on his side. He wanted Rommel attacked, beaten, and eliminated in Cyrenaica before a likely German victory in Russia permitted Hitler to drive his Panzers across the Caucasus towards the Persian Gulf and the Red Sea. This is precisely what the Wehrmacht was planning to do.

Malta reinforced

The new delay to "Crusader" had no adverse effect on the progress of the operations, thanks to the pressure exerted on Axis communications in the Mediterranean by the sea and naval air forces of Admirals Cunningham and Somerville. No harm can be done to these remarkable

▽ *A picture from one of a series of posters on the rôle of the Merchant Navy in the war. It claimed that out of every 200 ships that sailed in convoy, 199 arrived safely. In the Mediterranean, however, where shipping came under attack from the air and from Italian and German submarines, the losses were so high that Tobruk had to be supplied by fast warships at night, and organising convoys for Malta became a major naval operation.*

commanders' reputations by pointing out two circumstances which made their task easier. In the first place, after the Balkans campaign X *Fliegerkorps* did not return to its bases in Sicily but served with Rommel. In the second place, the Italian fleet was not permitted to operate beyond coastal waters. In these conditions, the three convoys sent to Malta during 1941 lost only one merchant ship out of the 40 which left Gibraltar. Force H came well out of these dangerous operations, losing only the cruiser *Southampton* and the destroyer *Fearless,* though the battleship Nelson was seriously damaged on the "Halberd" convoy in a torpedo attack by an audacious Italian pilot.

In the same period the aircraft-carrier *Ark Royal,* sometimes accompanied by the *Victorious,* despatched to Malta nearly 300 fighters, most of which reached their destination. Also, during the summer, the island's airfields were reoccupied by a small attacking force of Blenheim and Wellington bombers. Finally, on October 21, Captain W. G. Agnew's Force K–the light cruisers *Aurora* and *Penelope,* from Scapa Flow–anchored in the Grand Harbour. The situation around Malta now seemed sufficiently under control for the Admiralty to send the cruisers *Ajax* and *Neptune* to join them a few weeks later.

This succession of reinforcements explains why, from August onwards, supplies to the Axis forces in Libya became more and more unreliable. During September, 94,000 tons of equipment and fuel were loaded in Italy, but 26,000 tons of it went to the bottom. Submarines operating from Malta took the lion's share of this destruction. For example, on September 18 Commander Wanklyn in *Upholder* sank with five torpedoes two 19,500 ton ships *Oceania* and *Neptunia.* Also taking part in this sea offensive were the Alexandria and Gibraltar flotillas, including two Dutch vessels.

The Italian defence was at a disadvantage in this fighting since their vessels had no asdic of the type used by British escorts. A few dozen sets were obtained from Germany during the summer of 1941, but it took time for them to be installed and crews trained to use them, time which was not wasted by their opponents. On the other hand, minefields in waters around Malta and Tripoli accounted for five of the eight British submarines lost in the Mediterranean in 1941.

In October, losses of supplies between Italian ports and Tripolitania amounted to one fifth of the cargoes loaded, and of 12,000 tons of fuel bound for the Axis forces, 2,500 tons disappeared into the sea. November was even worse, and for a while it was thought that Rommel would be brought to a standstill. In fact, out of a

▷ *Polish troops of General S. Kopanski's 1st Carpathian Brigade embark in Alexandria for Tobruk. During periods of the new moon in September and October they were shipped with the British 70th Division. The 9th Australian Division and the 18th Infantry Brigade Group were evacuated. The operation, which was the result of political pressure from Australia, forced Auchinleck to postpone Operation "Crusader" for over a fortnight.*

▽ *An Australian picket seated on one of the robust anti-tank obstacles which made up the Tobruk defences.*

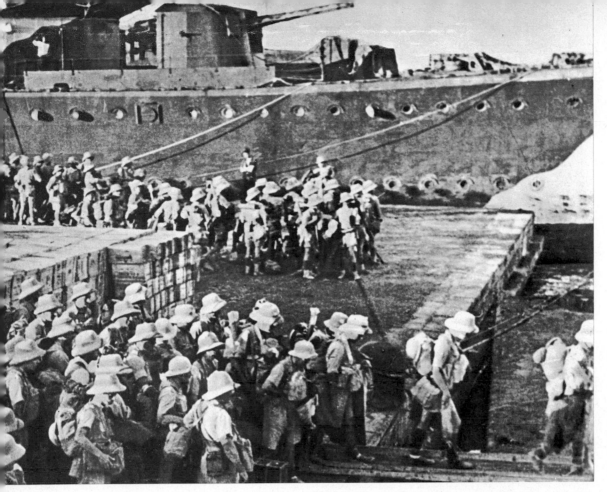

total of 79,208 tons of supplies loaded in Italy, he lost 62 per cent (49,365 tons). Every episode in the first battle of the convoys cannot be described here, but the disaster of November 9 does deserve mention in some detail.

The convoy "*Duisburg*", composed of six merchant ships and a tanker, left Messina on the afternoon of November 8. It was closely escorted by six destroyers, backed up by the 3rd Cruiser Squadron commanded by Vice-Admiral Brivonesi (*Trento*, *Trieste*, and four destroyers). At 1645 the convoy was sighted and reported to Malta by a Maryland on patrol. At nightfall Captain Agnew set out with his cruisers and the destroyers *Lance* and *Lively*. Other aircraft, in constant radar contact with the enemy, guided him to the convoy.

Nine sinkings in ten minutes

Towards 0100, about 155 miles east of Syracuse, the convoy appeared on the radar screens of the British ships, themselves still unseen by the Italians. Less than ten minutes later it was all over, after a barrage of shellfire and torpedoes. The seven merchant ships were sinking,

and the destroyer *Fulmine* was going down with them, shattered by a salvo from the *Aurora*. The attack had been so rapid that the 3rd Cruiser Squadron, in any case badly equipped for battle at night, had not time to intervene. On top of all this, near dawn, the destroyer *Libeccio* was sunk by the tireless *Upholder*.

With losses mounting, *Supermarina* tried to ensure delivery of the fuel vital to the Libyan operations by using very fast light cruisers. As a result of this decision, there was another disaster during the night of December 13. Loaded with drums of oil, the cruisers *Alberico da Barbiano* and *Alberto di Guissano* had sailed for Tripoli from Palermo. They were sighted by Malta-based aircraft which transmitted the information to Commander G. H. Stokes, leading four destroyers, including the Dutch vessel *Isaac Sweers*, from Gibraltar to Alex-

andria. Stokes surprised the two Italian ships off Cape Bon. Their cargo caught fire immediately and most of their crews, including Admiral Toscano, perished. And as if this were not enough, during the same night two brand new merchant ships, *Filzi* and *Del Greco,* were sunk.

In short, post-war statistics show that in the second half of 1941 Italy lost no less than 189 merchant vessels totalling 500,000 tons. On June 10, 1940, taking into account 500,000 tons of Italian shipping frozen in American ports, the Italian merchant fleet had totalled 3,300,000 tons. As a result of these losses, the situation for the Italians by the middle of December was, to say the least, very serious.

Was *Supermarina* betrayed?

When one considers these events, so disastrous for the Axis, the question arises whether they were due to treason committed by a member of *Supermarina* in a key position. This question caused violent arguments in Italy, and ended in the courts. In his book *The Foxes of the Desert,* Paul Carell supports this view, but such serious naval historians as Bragadin and Admiral Bernotti refute it. Methodical modern techniques of enquiry, using evidence from continuous monitoring of enemy radio communica-

◁ ◁ *Force H on the move, the battle cruiser* Renown, *the* Ark Royal, *and the cruiser* Sheffield *ready for action near Gibraltar.*
△ △ *An Italian convoy forms up in the shelter of a friendly coast line. The Italian Navy, which was responsible for the security of these convoys lacked adequate fuel stocks to do this and conduct offensive operations against the Royal Navy.*
△ *Three cruisers of the Royal Italian Navy under attack by British aircraft in the Mediterranean.*

tions, tend to leave one sceptical of the theory. Moreover, there were one or more British submarines permanently on the watch outside every port where convoys were formed. Finally, the two incidents already described are proof of the excellent work done by reconnaissance aircraft, operating from Malta with complete impunity.

The French contribution

Italian ships bound for Tripoli had been used to hugging the Tunisian coast in order to avoid the perils waiting for them in the open sea. Thus they were spotted by French observers, who had already carefully recorded the wreckage of Axis units washed ashore at Kerkenna after

the battle on April 15 and had also been the first to report the movement of the 15th Panzer Division to Africa. General de Gaulle's men were no longer the only ones passing information to the British. General Weygand, in his memoirs, reveals that Major Navarre, his head of Intelligence, had organised a secret Intelligence system to transmit as quickly as possible the information about Axis convoy movements to Tripolitania obtained on the Tunisian coast by air and naval observers. He was to continue this activity although General Weygand was relieved of his post as the government's Delegate-General in Africa and replaced by General Juin on November 18, 1941.

Cavallero seeks to occupy Tunisia

Marshal Cavallero, Chief-of-Staff at *Comando Supremo,* had not waited until disaster was inevitable before grasping the importance of the port of Bizerta and Tunisian lines of communication. At a meeting at Brenner on June 2 he made his views known to Field-Marshal Keitel. His German colleague was very cool on this question, considering that Cavallero's inclination for strong action would result in the secession of the French Empire, whereas by bargaining with prisoners-of-war and by negotiation, Vichy should be amenable to further concessions. This was also Hitler's view.

The hunters, the team that made Malta a constant threat to Axis convoys in the Mediterranean.
△ ◁ *The submarines* Taku *(foreground),* Una *(left), and* Unrivalled *(right). In addition to offensive operations, submarines lurked at the entrance of major Italian ports gathering information about convoys and naval activity.*
◁ ◁ *The* Penelope *enters Valletta. Launched in 1935 she served in the Mediterranean and Home Fleets, and was sunk early in 1944. As part of Force K, she reached Malta on October 21, 1941.*
△ *A Bristol Blenheim Mk IV. Blenheims, Marylands, and Wellingtons based on Malta, in conjunction with aircraft of the Fleet Air Arm, sunk 115,000 tons of Axis shipping between June and October 1941.*

▷ *Sinking slowly by the stern, an Italian freighter is caught in the shadow of a circling British aircraft. She was sunk by aircraft based at Malta as she worked along the Tunisian coast towards Tripoli.*

▽ *Life boats are swung out, and a sailor jumps overboard (bottom right) as R.A.F. Blenheims scream in over an Italian timber vessel. Post-war figures showed that Italy lost 189 merchant vessels totalling 500,000 tons, much of it to the fatally efficient team of submarines, surface vessels, and aircraft based on Malta.*

▷▷ *Afrika Korps soldiers with a captured British truck. The soldier on the right also has a British water bottle.*

Count Ciano met Admiral Darlan at Turin on December 9 and gave no support to the *Comando Supremo*. When Darlan brought up the question of the Tunisian ports the Duce's son-in-law cut him short. He wrote: "I interrupted him to say that I had no intention of talking about this subject and had no instructions to do so." There is no satisfactory explanation for Ciano's negative attitude, so clearly prejudicial to the campaign then being fought.

Rommel's secrecy

Since his victory at Sollum-Halfaya, Rommel had nurtured plans to capture Tobruk. The successes of Force K and Malta-based R.A.F. operations, however, forced him to postpone the attack from week to week. By November 4 everything was at last ready, and he revealed his plans to Marshal Cavallero in Rome.

To take advantage of the full moon, the operation would begin between November 20 and December 4. The evening before the chosen day, the "Brescia" Division would make a strong diversionary attack on the south-west front, thus drawing the defence's reinforcements. The following dawn Rommel would attack the fortress from the south-east with General Crue-well's *Afrika Korps* and General Navarrini's Italian XXI Corps. He calculated that it would be all over in 48 hours.

After the meeting, Cavallero wrote: "I asked Rommel if he thought the enemy might be able to launch a full-scale attack. He thought not because the enemy would not want to expose their lines of communication to easier interception by the German and Italian divisions. He expected defensive action by relatively few ground forces but with air support."

Was Rommel unaware of General Auchinleck's offensive preparations or did he conceal them from the Italian Chief-of-Staff in case he should be ordered to remain on the defensive? In 1949 this was still an open question, and in the Italian official account we read:

"There was a striking difference in the information supplied by the German and Italian Intelligence services. For reasons that were not very clear, the Germans insisted that the British had no intention of taking the offensive, and considered their Italian colleagues to be 'excessively nervous Latins'." Again, on November 11, Major von Mellenthin, chief of Rommel's Intelligence, discussing the matter with an Italian liaison officer, said: "Major Revetria (chief of Italian Intelligence) is too jumpy. Tell him to calm down, because the British are not going to attack."

In 1955, however, Mellenthin, in his war memoirs, gave the key to the enigma, writing quite candidly: "To allay the fears of the Italians and prevent interference with his plans, Rommel instructed his staff to adopt a confident tone in all discussions with Italian officers, and in November—as the date of our attack drew nearer—I deliberately minimised the possibilities of a British offensive whenever I spoke to our allies."

CHAPTER 53
Operation "Crusader"

Sir Claude Auchinleck had organised the troops taking part in "Crusader" into the 8th Army, commanded by Lieutenant-General Sir Alan Cunningham, who had just achieved fame for his lightning defeat of the Italians in Abyssinia. Auchinleck had thus some justification for giving him precedence over his colleague Sir Henry Maitland Wilson, in spite of Churchill's disagreement. He had no idea that Cunningham would not be equal to the strain involved in directing a battle between armoured forces. On the day of the battle the 8th Army was deployed as follows:

Tobruk:
70th Division (Major-General R. M. Scobie, who also commanded the whole garrison); Polish 1st Carpathian Infantry Brigade Group (Major-General S. Kopanski); and 32nd Army Tank Brigade (Brigadier A. C. Willison);

Right flank:
XIII Corps (Lieutenant-General A. R.

△ *A fighting patrol returns through the Tobruk perimeter wire. The aggressive garrison was a constant irritant to Rommel, who was preparing to attack the fortress when Operation "Crusader" broke on his main front on November 18, 1941. Many of the defences at Tobruk had been built by the Italians and were captured intact in the early months of the desert war. They were soundly built and resisted both their former owners and the Afrika Korps.*

▷ *Italian anti-aircraft guns in garrison had no aircraft of their own, support missions were flown from the main British lines, and the Royal Navy brought in the essential supplies that kept the men alive and fighting.*

Godwin-Austen), made up of:
1. New Zealand Division (Major-General B. C. Freyberg);
2. 4th Indian Division (Major-General F. W. Messervy); and
3. 1st Army Tank Brigade (Brigadier H. R. B. Watkins); and

Left flank:
XXX Corps (Lieutenant-General C. W. M. Norrie), made up of:
1. 7th Armoured Division (Major-General W. H. E. Gott);
2. 4th Armoured Brigade Group (Brigadier A. H. Gatehouse);
3. 1st South African Division (Major-General G. L. Brink); and
4. 22nd Guards Brigade (Brigadier J. C. O. Marriott).

This was a completely motorised and partially armoured force, spearheaded by the 7th Armoured Division. The "Desert Rats" had 473 tanks–310 Crusaders and 163 American M3 Stuarts.

The British had by no means given up using tanks as infantry support weapons, so the Tobruk garrison and XIII Corps each included an independent brigade equipped with either cruiser or Matilda tanks. In all, 8th Army had 724 tanks at the front and could count on 200 more in reserve to replace any losses.

In the air, Air Vice-Marshal H. Coningham provided the 8th Army with support from the Western Desert Air Force's 16 fighter, eight bomber, and three reconnaissance squadrons. Finally there was Sir Andrew Cunningham, whose fleet's guns were there to give direct support to his brother's operations. This explains the British soldier's characteristically humorous nickname for the operation– "Cunningham, Cunningham, and Coningham".

The Axis deployment might give the impression that Rommel's armour was under the command of General Ettore Bastico and that the "Italian Supreme Commander in North Africa" could control General Gambara's XX Corps. But the impetuous *Panzergruppe Afrika* commander had no intention whatsoever of respecting this chain of command, and went over Bastico's head to appeal directly to the *Comando Supremo,* or even to Hitler, when he did not agree with Cavallero's decisions. The deployment was as follows, under Bastico's overall command:
1. Italian XX Mobile Corps (General Gambara), made up of:
   a. "Ariete" Armoured Division

(General Balotta) and
   b. "Trieste" Motorised Division (General Piazzoni); and
2. *Panzergruppe Afrika* (Rommel), made up of:
   i *Afrika Korps* (Lieutenant-General Ludwig Cruewell), composed of:
      a. 15th Panzer Division (Major-General Walther Neumann-Silkow);
      b. 21st Panzer Division (Major-General Johann von Ravenstein);
      c. *Afrika* Division (Major-General Sommermann); and
      d. "Savona" Division (General de Giorgis); and
   ii Italian XXI Corps (General Enea Navarrini), composed of:
      a. "Brescia' Division (General Zambon);
      b. "Trento" Division (General de Stefanis);
      c. "Bologna" Division (General Gloria); and
      d. "Pavia' Division (General Franceschini).

Panzergruppe Afrika was formed on August 15 and this enabled Rommel to hand over command of the *Afrika Korps* to General Cruewell. The 5th Light Division was renamed 21st Panzer Division, but retained its original composition. The *Afrika* Division comprised only two infantry battalions, recruited from former German volunteers in the French Foreign Legion, to whom Hitler

Sir Alan Cunningham was born in 1887. In December 1940, as G.O.C. East Africa Force, he commanded the troops who marched against the coastal towns of Italian Somaliland and then the 1,000-mile drive on the Abyssinian capital of Addis Ababa. This operation was notable for the skill he showed in using his force's mobility and the low loss of life. In August 1941 Cunningham took command of the new 8th Army which with 30,000 vehicles was almost entirely mechanised. In the offensive of November he suffered heavy tank losses and wished to break off the action. General Auchinleck did not agree and on the 26th he was replaced by General Ritchie. Tobruk, the objective of the offensive, was relieved in December.

△ *Major-General Ronald Scobie, garrison commander at Tobruk.*

▷ *Lieutenant-General Ludwig Cruewell, who assumed command of the* Afrika Korps *with Rommel's promotion to the command of* Panzergruppe Afrika. *During the chaotic fighting that took place in the "Crusader" operation he lost contact with Rommel, and narrowly escaped capture by the 6th New Zealand Brigade, but the documents, headquarters equipment, and most of the staff of the* Afrika Korps *were captured on the dawn of November 23.*

was offering a chance to "make good". At the beginning of December it was renamed the 90th Light Division.

While the Italian XXI Corps was to overrun Tobruk, the *Afrika Korps*—some German units and the whole "Savona" Division—would make contact with the British on the Sidi Omar–Capuzzo–Halfaya–Sollum front. Ready for any eventuality, the 15th and 21st Panzer Divisions were stationed in the Gambut area and further south. Finally, Gambara had placed the "Ariete" Armoured Division around the Bir el Gubi watering place and the "Trieste" Motorised Division around Bir Hakeim.

The Axis forces thus amounted to ten divisions, against the 8th Army's six divisions. But it should not be overlooked that the large Italian units were considerably under-strength and that Rommel's supplies of food and fuel were more and more uncertain. As for the armoured forces, General Cunningham had 724

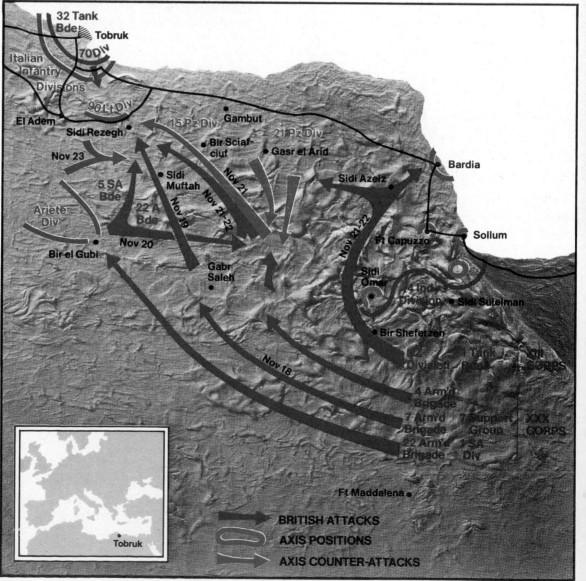

BRITISH ATTACKS
AXIS POSITIONS
AXIS COUNTER-ATTACKS

tanks, the Italians 189, and the Germans 249.

These are the approximate figures of the forces involved. But when one gets down to brass tacks the British superiority was reduced by certain technical factors. No doubt the 189 tanks in the "Ariete" Armoured Division were of no great consequence, and General Cruewell's 69 Pzkw II tanks were no better. The latent defects of the Matilda are well known, and the Crusaders and other cruisers were subject to frequent mechanical faults. In addition the Stuart or M3, driven by an aero engine requiring a high octane fuel, displayed an alarming tendency to catch fire.

But this is not all. Whereas none of the British tanks had weapons more powerful than 40-mm (37-mm for the American M3), half of the *Afrika Korps'* 136 Pzkw III's were fitted with a 5-cm rather than 3.7-cm gun, and their 31 Pzkw IV's already had a 7.5-cm. Ballistically, the heavier the projectile the more consistent its speed, giving it a longer range and a greater armour-piercing potential. With their $4\frac{1}{2}$-pounder (5-cm) and 15-pounder (7.5-cm) shells, the Germans had an important advantage over their opponents' 40-mm shells, weighing only two pounds.

On the tactical level, it appears that the Germans had struck a better balance between tanks, infantry, and artillery than the 8th Army, and that their radio communications were more reliable. One should also remember Rommel's formidable defensive weapon – the 8·8-cm anti-aircraft gun.

Cunningham's preparations

According to Cunningham's plans, the leading rôle in "Crusader" was to be played by XXX Corps, which would cross the Egyptian-Libyan border near

▽ *Pzkw III's on the move in the desert. Their 5-cm guns gave them a distinct advantage in the tank versus tank contests fought at long range in North Africa. Such battles resembled naval actions in which the opponents met and manoeuvred over a vast level area. In fighting in which there was no real "front line", commanders needed good communications and a reliable supply of fuel and ammunition – they were also in danger of being captured by advanced enemy units.*

◁ In a propaganda photograph an Italian M.C. 200 Saetta flies beside a German Bf 110 fighter. Co-operation between the Axis partners in the Mediterranean was with some notable exceptions fairly successful. The Saetta was used as an escort to Luftwaffe bombers and saw action over Malta, North Africa and the Mediterranean, as well as Greece and Yugoslavia. But the bulk of operations against the British 8th Army fell to the Luftwaffe.

▷ A Stuka's eye view of Tobruk. The fortress was bombarded from the air and the ground, and rations and supplies had to be brought in at night in a perilous journey in which destroyers worked through a maze of sunken shipping in the harbour. When Goebbels spoke of the garrison as "the Rats of Tobruk", describing their subterranean day-time life, they were flattered by this interest, and took the insult as their nickname.

▽ A battery of 17-cm guns opens fire. Rommel once said that the desert was "the tactician's paradise and the quartermaster's hell": each side suffered from supply problems, but the Germans had the additional disadvantage of being equipped with captured Russian and British guns, all of different calibres.

▽ An MG 34 dug in in the sustained fire rôle. The profile of the weapon has been lowered by recessing the tripod legs. If a position was well dug, the desert heat haze would make it invisible except at close range. The first "general purpose machine gun" as we now know them, the MG 34 was used in tanks, and also as an anti-aircraft gun. It had a rate of fire of between 800 and 900 rounds per minute, though later models reached 1,000 rounds per minute.

△ *A British Crusader Mk. 1 stops by a burning German Pzkw IV tank during the opening stages of Operation "Crusader". Though the Crusader was admired by the Germans for its high speed (it could reach, and sometimes better, 27 m.p.h.) it was no match for the Panzers with its 2-pdr gun and thin armour. The Pzkw IV had armour up to 50-mm thick and a 7.5-cm gun with a 15-pdr shell.*

Fort Maddalena and deploy at Gabr Saleh. It was expected that while this was happening, Rommel would have arrived, and a tank battle would then take place, in which the more numerous and better equipped British and South Africans would have the upper hand. Meanwhile, from the south-east, XIII Corps would overrun the frontier position at Sollum–Sidi Omar. With the *Afrika Korps* toppled, XXX Corps would push on vigorously to Sidi Rezegh to join up with the Tobruk garrison, which, on the signal, would break out of the Italian XXI Corps' partial encirclement to meet the British forces advancing from the south-east.

Between Cunningham's two columns, however, there was a 20-mile gap, which would widen as Godwin-Austen's XIII Corps moved north and Norrie's XXX Corps headed north-west. Fearing an outflanking movement on his left, Godwin-Austen therefore demanded, and secured, an intermediary column, which was drawn, however, from Norrie's force. Norrie was far from pleased with this decision which, in the event, was an unfortunate one. The resulting diversion

of the 4th Armoured Brigade meant that the 7th Armoured Division lost a third of its strength, 165 Stuarts, and was thus weakened in what was intended to be its decisive rôle.

This was the first setback to the operation, even before it had begun. When the attack got under way at dawn on November 18, in torrential rain, Rommel's reaction caused a second setback. Ready to attack Tobruk, he saw the British move as no more than a reconnaissance in strength and kept his armoured forces around Gambut, whereas Cunningham was waiting for him at Gabr Saleh. On top of all this, a third setback occurred with the capture of no less than the 8th Army operations orders, carelessly brought to the front by a British officer. This happened on November 19 when the 22nd Armoured Brigade, equipped with the new Crusader tanks (7th Armoured Division) was defeated in its attempt to take Bir el Gubi, bitterly defended by the "Ariete" Armoured Division. This fourth setback cost the British about 50 tanks.

XXX Corps did, however, reach Sidi

The British Crusader I Cruiser Tank Mk. VI (A15)

Weight: 19 tons.
Crew: 5.
Armament: one 2-pdr gun with 110 rounds and two 7.92-mm Besa machine guns (one coaxial with the main armament and one in an auxiliary turret, often removed, in the nose of the vehicle) with 4,500 rounds, and one .303-inch Bren machine gun with 600 rounds.
Armour: hull front 30-mm, driver's hood 40-mm, glacis 20-mm, nose 33-mm, sides 28-mm, rear 28-mm, top 7-mm, floor 10-mm, turret front 40-mm, sides 24-mm, rear 30-mm, and top 12-mm.
Engine: Nuffield Liberty 12-cylinder V, 340-hp.
Speed: 27 plus mph.
Range: 200 miles.
Length: 19 feet 7 inches.
Width: 9 feet 1 inch.
Height: 7 feet 4 inches.

Rezegh, although weakened for the reasons already explained. There it met a counter-attack by the *Afrika Korps*, strengthened by the Italian XXI Corps, ordered in by Mussolini himself at Rommel's direct request. Sunday, November 23 was a black day for Willoughby Norrie. His 5th South African Brigade lost Sidi Rezegh, and its commander was taken prisoner. The 7th Armoured Division suffered losses of 200 tanks and the capture of Brigadier Sperling, whose 4th Armoured Brigade had been given a rough handling by the 5th Panzer Regiment of the 21st Panzer Division.

If Rommel had followed up this important success against XXX Corps he could probably have wiped it out. But this chance was not enough for him; he was after the destruction of the whole of 8th Army. To do this, he brought 15th and 21st Panzer Divisions under his direct command, left Lieutenant-Colonel Siegfried Westphal, head of the operations section, in charge of the *Panzergruppe* H.Q., and set off with his Chief-of-Staff, Major-General Alfred Gause, and 100 tanks to reach the Mediterranean by way of Sidi Omar and strike the British in the rear.

▽ *Ignoring a dead crewman, a British soldier examines a captured Pzkw IV. Rommel lost 142 of the 249 tanks which he commanded at the beginning of "Crusader". 32,000 prisoners, 9,000 of them Germans, were taken in two months by the 8th Army, which itself lost only 8,000 men. It was a victory for the 8th Army, but one which they were unable to follow up. Another two years of thrust and parry would be needed before the Afrika Korps finally surrendered at Cape Bon.*

◁ *Huddled in a shell scrape,
(a shallow and very temporary
weapon pit) the crew of a Vickers
machine gun opens fire in the
chilly desert dawn. The Vickers
machine gun was nearly 57 years
old in 1939, and with some small
modifications it would soldier
on to 1965. It was awkward,
heavy, and cumbersome, but
utterly reliable. It needed 7½ pints
of water to cool the barrel, and
this presented an additional
supply problem in the desert.*

Auchinleck perseveres

For Cunningham, in his Maddalena H.Q.,
the reversals occurring since November
19 and the strain they imposed would
have been sufficient justification for the
order to retreat. But in the evening of the
23rd, Sir Claude Auchinleck appeared
in his mobile caravan H.Q. and ordered
him to continue the attack. Auchinleck
later wrote: "My opinion was different
from Cunningham's. I thought Rommel
was probably in as bad shape as we were,
especially with Tobruk unvanquished
behind him, and I ordered the offensive
to continue. I certainly gambled (in fact,
by going on we might have lost all) and
Cunningham might very well have proved
to be right and I wrong!"

At the same moment, his opponent,
writing to his wife, claimed to be "well,
in excellent spirits and full of confidence."
In spite of this, Rommel's raid in the
British rear did not succeed in upsetting
Auchinleck. "He is making a desperate
effort but he won't get very far," he said
to Cunningham on November 24. At the
end of his order of the day to his troops
he told them:

"His position is desperate, and he is
trying by lashing out in all directions to
distract us from our object, which is to
destroy him utterly. We will NOT be
distracted and he WILL be destroyed.
You have got your teeth into him. Hang
on and bite deeper and deeper and hang
on till he is finished. Give him NO rest.
The general situation in NORTH AFRICA
is EXCELLENT. There is only one order:
ATTACK AND PURSUE. ALL OUT
EVERYONE."

But as he suspected that Cunningham
was in no condition to carry out this
aggressive plan, he replaced him, on
November 26, by his own Deputy Chief-of-
Staff, Major-General Neil Methuen
Ritchie. The former chief of Intelligence
in the *Panzergruppe Afrika,* in his book
Panzer Battles, said of this action by
Auchinleck at this most critical moment:
"This was certainly one of the most
important decisions of the war. Auchinleck's will to attack and his strategy of
penetration saved 'Crusader' and much
else besides." This is a sound judgement.

Although Ritchie took over from
Cunningham it was Auchinleck who
directed the battle.

△ A 15-cm gun in action. The siege of Tobruk absorbed much of the Axis heavy artillery then available in North Africa.
▷ △ Victors in Operation "Crusader", a group of British soldiers display a tattered Swastika flag on top of a captured Pzkw IV.
▷ ▽ A 15-cwt truck of the 8th Army's XXX Corps reaches the Libyan border with Egypt. Both sides used captured armoured and soft-skinned vehicles.

On November 25 Scobie received a telegram informing him that the New Zealand Division would attempt to take Sidi Rezegh the next day. The garrison was then expected to occupy El Duda. Scobie launched a new attack on the morning of November 26. After a fierce struggle his infantry overcame the final centre of resistance called "Wolf". But there was still no sign of the arrival of the New Zealanders. At 1300 hours the garrison saw tanks on the horizon, and from one of their turrets three red rockets soared into the blue sky.

The troops cheered wildly, for it was the recognition signal of the 8th Army. Reinforcements were at last in sight!

Rommel decides to retreat

Writing to his wife on their silver anniversary, Rommel described his action behind the British lines as a "magnificent success" calling for a "special communiqué" from O.K.W. But he was undoubtedly alone in this view. For not only

had he not overcome the 4th Indian Division's stubborn resistance or captured the 8th Army's supply dumps, but he had also left the *Panzergruppe* without orders for four days, unconcerned that a few hours after his reckless departure he had lost his mobile radio, broken down in the desert.

Liddell Hart's description of this incident in his presentation of Rommel's notebooks gives some idea of the life led in the desert by the commanders themselves:

"A wireless signal from Rommel summoned the commander of the Afrika Korps to the Panzer Group's forward H.Q., which was said to be located near Gambut. After searching for a long time in the darkness they finally discovered a British lorry, which General Cruewell's command car approached with great caution. Inside it, to his good fortune, were no British troops, but Rommel and his Chief of Staff, both of whom were unshaven, worn with lack of sleep and caked with dust. In the lorry was a heap of straw as a bed, a can of stale water to drink and a few tins of food. Close by were two wireless trucks and a few dispatch riders. Rommel now gave his instructions for next day's operations."

Meanwhile, XIII Corps had succeeded where XXX Corps had failed. The New Zealand Division, moving through Belhamed, had made contact with the Tobruk garrison, which itself had broken out at El Duda.

With the situation becoming more critical, Lieutenant-Colonel Westphal took it upon himself to pass over the head of his untraceable chief and recall to the Tobruk sector the 21st Panzer Division, which was unattached south of Sollum. When he returned to his H.Q. on November 27, Rommel tacitly endorsed this initiative and without any pause mounted a new operation designed to bring him victory. Some very confused engagements followed, during which the New Zealand Division was cut in two and part of it thrown back to Tobruk. The Germans were becoming exhausted, however, and the 21st Panzer Division's commander, General von Ravenstein, was captured in the confusion.

Auchinleck's reinforcement of the 8th Army had been timely, and the rapidly reorganised XXX Corps again made its presence felt in the battle. Rommel, on the other hand, had to rely on only a

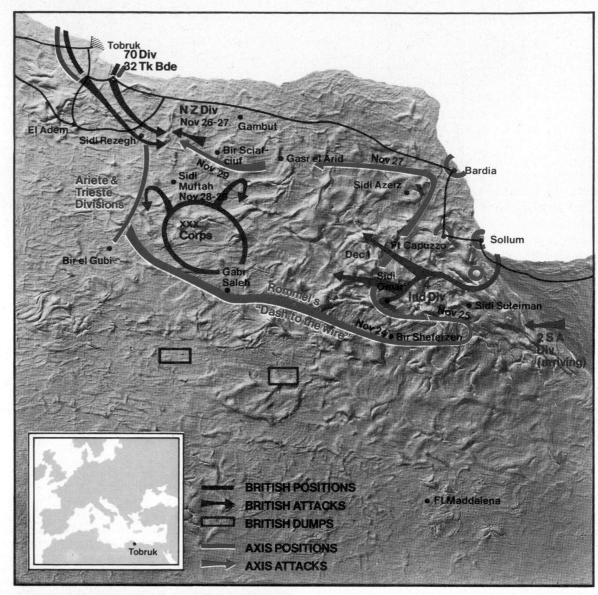

NZ Div
Nov 26-27
Gambut
Tobruk
70 Div
32 Tk Bde
El Adem
Sidi Rezegh
Bir Sciaf-
ciuf
Nov 29
Gasr el Arid
Nov 27
Bardia
Ariete &
Trieste
Divisions
Sidi
Muftah
Nov 28-2
Sidi Azerz
XXX
Corps
Ft Capuzzo
Sollum
Dec 1
Bir el Gubi
Sidi
Omar
Ind Div
Gabr
Saleh
Rommel's
"Dash to the wire"
Nov 25
Sidi Suleiman
Nov 24
Bir Sheferzen
2 SA
Div
(arriving)
F.t Maddalena
Tobruk

BRITISH POSITIONS
BRITISH ATTACKS
BRITISH DUMPS
AXIS POSITIONS
AXIS ATTACKS

▷ △ *A Bf 110 fighter lands in a
cloud of sand on an Italian-built
airfield in North Africa. All
engines suffered from the sand
and heat, but aero engines were
particularly vulnerable and
needed special filters.*
▷ ▽ *A standard bearer of
Jagdgeschwader 27 at a
ceremonial parade. It was in
this wing that Hans-Joachim
Marseille scored most of his 158
kills. Marseille was the 30th
ranking German ace.*
▽ *Luftwaffe medical orderlies
operating a water purification
plant. Fresh water was needed
for both men and vehicles and
little was available for washing.
Only sea bathing gave them a
chance for a complete clean-up.*

handful of tanks in the decisive days that
lay ahead. He had been warned that no
supplies of any consequence could be
delivered before the latter half of
December. So on December 5 he withdrew
his forces attacking east of Tobruk, and
the next day, after a counter-attack had
failed, gave the order for a general retreat.
He left to the "Savona" Division the
honour of holding out as long as possible
in the Bardia–Sollum–Halfaya area.

Axis disagreement

The previous summer, while waiting for
a British offensive, the Germans and
Italians had agreed to make an all-out
defensive stand on the heights of Aïn el
Gazala if it became impossible to hold
the frontier. General Bastico now wanted
to stick to this plan, as it had the advantage of covering Benghazi. Rommel, how-

ever, insisted that to stand on this line would risk the loss of Tripolitania without even saving Cyrenaica. In his view, as a result of British superiority, the retreat should be extended to Derna–Mechili; but he really wanted to move back to the area of Marsa Brega, which he had left on March 31.

On December 8, 14, and 17 these differences of opinion led to dramatic exchanges between the two commanders and their general staffs. During the first of these Rommel became excited and, according to the testimony of Lieutenant-Colonel Ravajoli exclaimed "that he had fought to win for three weeks, and that now he had decided to take his divisions to Tripoli and seek internment in Tunisia."

In order to win over the Italians to his argument in favour of a retreat he had no hesitation in using false information—now 2,000 or 3,000 motor vehicles sighted south of Sidi Barrani, now a convoy reported in Tobruk waters. On December 17 he succeeded in obtaining freedom of action from Cavallero, who had arrived with Field-Marshal Kesselring from Rome. One cannot blame Cavallero for not supporting his generals, since he knew that Rommel had gone over his head to obtain the approval of the Führer.

The British enter Benghazi

Whatever judgement one makes about Rommel's methods, the basic soundness of his decision must be admitted. Moreover he conducted the retreat in a masterly fashion, dealing sharp blows to the British whenever they became too hurried in pursuit. On Christmas Day, General Ritchie's advance guard entered Benghazi. But as the year ended, the 8th Army had not succeeded in intercepting

Rommel, although desert patrols had occupied the Jalo oasis. He was now securely in position behind the El Agheila –Marada strongpoint, leaving behind him 382 tanks destroyed since November 18. On January 17 the "Savona" Division, its food and ammunition exhausted, surrendered to General Villiers, commander of the 2nd South African Division, which had relieved the 4th Indian Division. 32,000 prisoners, 9,000 of them Germans, were taken by the 8th Army in two months. The 8th Army itself had lost 8,000 prisoners.

In Washington, Churchill was jubilant over this limited, but undeniable, victory. In a few weeks' time, he thought, Auchinleck would begin Operation "Acrobat", which would complete the destruction of the Axis forces in North Africa and take Ritchie from El Agheila to the Tunisian frontier. Then, under the agreement just reached with President Roosevelt, Operation "Gymnast" would be launched. With or without the consent of the Vichy Government, an Anglo-American expeditionary force would invade Morocco and Algeria.

Hitler reinforces the Mediterranean

For various reasons, the Mediterranean situation then changed, upsetting British plans.

First, Hitler was rightly concerned about the way things were developing and decided to send a submarine force there, just at the time when he seemed in sight of success in the battle of the Atlantic. From the outset, this move proved to be profitable, since on November 13 *U-81* (Lieutenant Guggenberger) sank the aircraft-carrier *Ark Royal* near

Gibraltar just after she had despatched another load of fighters to Malta. As *Illustrious*, *Formidable*, and *Indomitable* were still undergoing repairs in the United States, the only modern vessel in this class the Admiralty had was *Victorious*. Some 60 miles north of Sollum, *U-331* (Lieutenant von Tiesenhausen) succeeded in hitting the battleship *Barham* with three torpedoes, and this proud veteran of the Battle of Jutland disappeared in a terrible explosion, with 861 officers, petty officers, and men. Destroyers picked up 450 survivors, including Vice-Admiral Pridham-Wippell, who had distinguished himself at Cape Matapan. Finally, on December 14, not far from Alexandria, the light cruiser *Galatea* was destroyed by *U-557* (Lieutenant Paulsen).

Enter Kesselring

Hitler's assistance to his ally did not stop there. With the Italians' agreement he signed Directive No. 38 on December 2, ordering a unified command of the Axis forces in the central Mediterranean under a Supreme Commander "South" (*Oberbefehlshaber Süd*).

This was Field-Marshal Kesselring, commander of *Luftflotte* II. He was given a three-fold task:

"To win mastery of the air and sea in the area between Southern Italy and North Africa in order to ensure communications with Libya and Cyrenaica, and particularly to neutralise Malta. Secondly, to co-operate with the German and allied forces operating in North Africa. Thirdly, to paralyse enemy movements in the Mediterranean, including supplies to Tobruk and Malta, working in close co-operation with the available German and Italian naval forces."

Kesselring took command of the Luftwaffe air and anti-aircraft units already in the Mediterranean, and was reinforced by II *Fliegerkorps* (General Loerzer), withdrawn from the Eastern Front. So the Soviet allies obtained some benefit from British strategy between Malta and Suez.

But these were only half measures by Hitler, for the Supreme Commander "South", or O.B.S. as he was abbreviated, was nowhere in the same class as Eisenhower, Nimitz, or MacArthur when it came to commanding a whole theatre of war. In fact, *Panzergruppe Afrika* refused to acknowledge his supreme authority, thus very likely prejudicing the outcome of Axis operations. It remained to be proved that this Bavarian, a former artilleryman turned pilot, had a better overall conception of modern combined operations than the Württemberger, a former mountain infantryman converted to tanks. In addition, subordinate to the *Comando Supremo*, O.K.W., and even *Reichsmarschall* Göring, Kesselring's position was a most ambiguous one. In spite of all this, he was able to redress the balance in the central Mediterranean.

▽ *A British 7.2-inch howitzer in action near Tobruk. It was not until the second battle of El Alamein that British artillery would be used in numbers sufficient to allow centralised control: the 25-pounder was called upon to act as a long range anti-tank gun, while the communication and location system that allowed gunners to conduct effective counter-battery fire was dismantled. Artillery regiments were parcelled out to brigades, and batteries to defended localities.*

Aid from Japan

Japan's entry into World War II, especially the invasion of Malaya and the threat to Singapore, played its part in the changing fortunes in the Mediterranean. In Washington, the American President and the British Premier decided that, in spite of the Pearl Harbor and the Kuantan disasters, Germany was still to be considered as the prime enemy. Therefore, until Germany was beaten, the Allies would adopt an opportunist, wait-and-see policy in the Far East war. The Australian Government did not share this view. If Roosevelt could impose his own policy on Admiral Nimitz and General MacArthur, it did not follow that Churchill could do likewise with Mr. Curtin's troublesome government.

So the 6th and 7th Australian Divisions, which it had been hoped would take part in Operation "Acrobat", left the Middle East for good, and the British 70th Division embarked for Singapore. Again, the formation of a new squadron, to defend communications in the Indian Ocean against possible action by the Japanese fleet, prevented the Admiralty from making good the considerable losses sustained by the Mediterranean Fleet.

The naval balance begins to swing

During the night of December 18 and 19, Force K was pursuing an Italian convoy heading for North Africa when it ran into a minefield. *Neptune* struck four

△ *Field-Marshal Albert Kesselring, who as Supreme Commander "South" or O.B.S., was Rommel's superior. In his dealings with the Italians and the defence of southern Italy he was to prove himself both a diplomat and strategist; but Panzergruppe Afrika was reluctant to acknowledge his supreme authority. He is seen here leaving a Dornier Do 17 on a visit to Luftwaffe units in North Africa.*

The death of the Barham. Launched in December 1914, she served at Jutland in World War I and with the Home and Mediterranean Fleets in World War II. At 1629 on November 25 she was hit by three torpedoes from U-331, which had evaded the destroyer screen. She took on a severe list to the port and within a few minutes blew up with the loss of 861 officers and men, among them her commanding officer, Captain G. C. Cooke. This was the first British battleship to be sunk at sea and the loss was kept secret for several months. Losses from torpedoes, mines, and attack by frogmen left Cunningham with no more than four light cruisers and some destroyers at the end of December. Between November and December the Allies had lost five of their 33 capital ships and aircraft carriers, and a further eight would be out of commission for several months.

men slipped in behind a returning group of destroyers and aimed for their allotted targets: De la Penne and Bianchi for *Valiant,* Marceglia and Schergat for *Queen Elizabeth,* and Martellota and Marino for the large tanker *Sagona.* Once under the hulls of their targets, they removed the explosive warheads of their torpedoes, suspended them from the bottom of the vessels and set the detonators. All this was done in pitch darkness over 30 feet below the surface.

Sagona blew up first, at dawn on December 20. Then came *Valiant,* with De la Penne and Bianchi aboard. They had been picked up during the night but had uttered no word about their mission, of which they might have been the first victims. At about 0625 hours, Admiral Cunningham was on the rear deck of *Queen Elizabeth* inspecting the damage to *Valiant* when the explosion from Marceglia and Schergat's torpedo flung him four or five feet in the air.

As Roskill points out, "both battleships were seriously flooded and incapacitated for many months. Fortunately it was possible to keep them on even keels and the enemy's . . . air reconnaissance failed to reveal the full measure of success achieved." But it would be months before they rejoined the fleet, and meanwhile, apart from destroyers Cunningham had no more than four light cruisers under his command, including the old anti-aircraft cruiser *Carlisle.* The Italian Navy, thanks to its mines and midget submarines, had gained, in a single night, a considerable advantage in the Mediterranean. It is true, however, that it did not have enough supplies of oil fuel to make use of this advantage, and so the situation continued to deteriorate in 1942.

△ *"December 1941: All's well . . ." so reads the caption to this Illingworth cartoon. The attack on Pearl Harbor, which would give Japan temporary dominance in the Pacific, is discreetly shown in the bottom right of the globe. Even the German defeats in North Africa and Russia would be redressed in the spring offensives of 1942. But the supply of arms from the United States would grow with the defeat of the U-boat menace.*

mines in succession and sank with all her crew except one leading seaman. *Aurora* and *Penelope* survived, but were so badly damaged that they remained unseaworthy for many long weeks. The destroyer *Kandahar* made a courageous attempt to help *Neptune* but her stern was blown off by another mine and she sank on the spot.

Italian human torpedoes

Also on December 18, at 2100 hours, with admirable precision, the Italian submarine *Sciré* (Lieutenant Valerio Borghese) managed to launch three manned torpedoes less than one and a half miles from the lighthouse overlooking Alexandria's main channel. Seated astride their machines, in pairs, the six daring

Crisis point for Allied seapower

Taking a general view of all the theatres of operations, it can be concluded that between November 25 and December 20, 1941, the Anglo-American forces had lost five of their 33 major vessels, and eight others were out of commission for some months. It may be argued that aircraft-carriers were taking the place of battleships. This is no doubt true, but Japan led the field in this category, with ten to her nearest rival's eight.

CHAPTER 54
The raiders return

A careless word...

...A NEEDLESS SINKING

◁ A U-boat at large, running on the surface, taken from the front cover of an issue of Die Wehrmacht, the German forces magazine. The German propaganda machine made full use of the fact that the Kriegsmarine's U-boat arm was the only section of the Wehrmacht which was bidding fair to bring Britain to her knees.

△ "Careless talk" and its effects on the high seas–the constant British nightmare during World War II. Fears that convoy sailing details might leak out to the Germans were not helped by the growing skill of the "wolf-packs."

▽ The popular image of the U-boat took many forms, most of them appropriately sinister. Here the essential viciousness of submarine commerce war is given a comical twist by Olaf Gulbransson of Munich's Simplicissimus.

△ *Britain's Admiral Sir Percy Noble, who became C.-in-C., Western Approaches, in February 1941. His Admiralty brief was "the protection of trade, the routing and control of the outward and homeward-bound ocean convoys and measures to combat any attacks on convoys by U-boats or hostile aircraft within his command".*
▽ *Germany's Admiral Karl Dönitz.*
▷ *The end of a merchantman.*

In his memoirs, Winston Churchill sums up the strategic situation as he saw it at the end of 1941 thus:

"Amid the torrent of violent events one anxiety reigned supreme. Battles might be won or lost, enterprises might succeed or miscarry, territories might be gained or quitted, but dominating all our power to carry on the war, or even keep ourselves alive, lay our mastery of the ocean routes and the free approach and entry to our ports."

Though written after the war, these words are not the product of hindsight, but express exactly the feelings of the wartime British leader as he prepared to face up to the menace of the U-boats and the four-engined Focke-Wulf Fw 200 Condor; although this does not mean to say that all the measures he took to eliminate the threat were equally effective, as we shall have occasion to point out later. But Churchill was never the one to commit himself half-heartedly.

Churchill and the "Battle of the Atlantic"

Proof of this is contained in his order of March 6, 1941, concerning the conduct of what he called "The Battle of the Atlantic", for the purpose of waging which he established that same day a standing committee. This brought together three times a week representatives of the Transport Department of the Admiralty, and of the Ministries of Transport and Shipping. To this new body fell the task of recommending measures necessary "to defeat the attempt to strangle our food supplies and our connection with the United States."

The Prime Minister naturally expected that among the means that Germany would use to attain these objectives, would figure prominently the renewed bombing by the Luftwaffe of Clydeside, Merseyside, and the Bristol Channel, since this was where American war supplies were being landed—and where the unloading and distribution operations were falling further and further behind schedule. Furthermore, one and a half million tons of merchant shipping were lying idle for lack of repair. Churchill therefore ordered the immediate strengthening of anti-aircraft defences in all the west coast ports.

Germany's answer to "Lend-Lease"

And indeed, during the early days of March, it certainly looked as if Hitler and Göring were going to follow this strategy. The results were sobering.

On March 13 and 14, Clydeside, which up till then had got off rather lightly, was subjected to the merciless attacks of the Luftwaffe; in fact, so fierce were the attacks upon Greenock and Glasgow that some shipyards remained closed until June, and others even until November. This "second edition" of the Blitz reached its height between May 1 and May 7, when, for seven successive nights, German bombers implacably pounded Liverpool and the adjoining Merseyside ports. Not only were there 3,000 dead and wounded as a result; in addition, 69 of the 144 mooring bays were put out of action, and the unloading capacity of the area reduced by 75 per cent for some weeks after.

Thus the shattering effects of this aerial bombardment of western port installations, combined with the successes achieved on the high seas by U-boats, Focke-Wulf Condors, and the surface raiders, added up to an effective reply to the "Lend-Lease" law promulgated by President Roosevelt on March 11, 1941. And yet, from May 13 onwards, after one last massive attack on London, the Luftwaffe relaxed the pressure it had—especially over the past few months, when the western ports had been the chief victims—been exerting on Britain. Some 43,381 civilians had been killed and 50,856 seriously injured; but the respite thus granted by the calling-off of the bombing was to last more than three years, until the launching of the first V-1 flying bombs on June 13, 1944.

It is of course, true that the implementation of Operation "Barbarossa" inevitably entailed the transfer of the bulk of the Luftwaffe from the West to the East, if the Russian giant was to be laid low before the onset of winter. Nevertheless, writing about this piece of good fortune in his memoirs, Churchill affirmed that if the Germans had continued their attacks against Britain, the Battle of the Atlantic would have been even more tightly fought. And in 1954, discussing this aspect of the conflict, Captain S. W. Roskill, the Royal

The Short Sunderland flying-boats flown by R.A.F. Coastal Command were invaluable tools in the Battle of the Atlantic. The Sunderland had a normal range of 2,980 miles and could carry up to 2,000 lbs of bombs. It also bristled with defensive armament, so much so that it earned the respectful Luftwaffe nickname of fliegende Stachelschwein – "flying porcupine".
▷ A Sunderland circles protectively over a stricken merchantman.
▽ Back at base, a Sunderland is hauled out of the water for checks and maintenance.

Navy's official historian, asked this question:

"If Hitler, instead of attacking Russia, had concentrated the full weight of his air power against our commercial ports, our docks and dockyards, our unloading and storage facilities, our coastal shipping and river estuaries, and had he kept the might of the Luftwaffe so directed for months on end if need were, could this country have survived?"

British defences strengthened

At all events, the Prime Minister, confronted with the growing menace of the Focke-Wulf aircraft, gave top priority to equipping the Merchant Navy with anti-aircraft weapons, the Admiralty providing the necessary gun crews. In addition, Fighter Command was given orders to release 50 fighters and pilots for convoy escort duty; these planes were to be installed on catapults on board merchantmen, from which they would take off on sighting a Condor; they would shoot it down and then ditch in the sea themselves, there to wait until one of the escort vessels came to pick them up – a procedure which inevitably resulted in the loss of the aircraft, and, very often, in that of the pilot's life. When escort aircraft-carriers, intended for convoy duty, came into operation, these expensive Catapult Aircraft Merchantmen were abandoned.

Facing up to Admiral Dönitz's U-boats in June 1941, the British defences were better equipped than a year earlier, thanks to the successful carrying out of the war production programme, and also to the additional help of the U.S.A. At his Liverpool base, where he had taken over command of Western Approaches on February 17, Sir Percy Noble had available for convoy escort duties 248 destroyers (59 of which were, in fact, being refitted and therefore unusable), 99 corvettes (small ships of 950 tons, admirably suited to this task, but the last word in discomfort), 48 sloops (ten of which had been recently transferred by Washington under the recent "Lend-Lease" Act, for the duration of hostilities), and 300 miscellaneous small craft. It should be noted, however, that as a result of the arduous tasks they were called upon to perform, a large proportion of them were out of action at any one time.

The escort vessels were fitted with the first radar equipment, which, though rather primitive, was quite effective in countering the enemy submarines' favourite tactic–the night surface attack. We are thus poised on the threshold of that escalation of this campaign, in which the last word went to the Allies.

Coastal Command's task

Though still part of the R.A.F., Coastal Command was placed under the operational control of the Admiralty from April 1941: a hybrid solution which goes far to explaining why Coastal Command was always at the end of the queue when it came to receiving new equipment, whether produced at home or supplied by the United States. A second explanation is

and the North Sea, to observe and harry German ships sheltering in Brest harbour, to lay mines, and to weed out raiders operating in the Atlantic. In short, July 1941 saw Air Chief-Marshal Sir Philip Joubert de la Ferté, who had just taken over from Sir Frederick Brownlow as the head of Coastal Command, having to carry out a great variety of tasks with insufficient resources.

At the same time, R.A.F. Coastal Command's Short Sunderland and Consolidated PBY Catalina flying boats, as well as Lockheed Hudson bombers, were being fitted with radar, sometimes combined with a searchlight.

The wrong targets

While Bomber Command made futile efforts to knock out German submarines

▽ *In the U-boat base at Lorient on the Biscay coast; one of the "grey wolves" is overhauled on the slip.*

that top priority was being given to Bomber Command, which was expected by the Chief of Air Staff, Sir Charles Portal, by the Air Minister, Sir Archibald Sinclair, and by the Prime Minister to cripple German industrial production, especially the submarine shipyards, in an impossibly short space of time.

In any case, the fight against the U-boat menace, though a high priority, was only one of the tasks which Coastal Command had to carry out. It had also to attack enemy shipping in the Channel

lying at their bases–Bremen, Hamburg, and Kiel–it proceeded to ignore the U-boat shelters then being built at Lórient, Saint Nazaire, Brest, la Pallice, and Bordeaux, which might have been more profitable targets. When, via the Free French "Rémy" network, Lieutenant Philippon sent a message from Brest to London, pointing out the magnitude of the work being carried out, and how important it was to attack these sites, London loftily replied, according to Jacques Mordal: "These bases will be attacked when they

With the U-boat service.
◁ Proud moment: The Reich War Banner is hoisted for the first time as a new U-boat is commissioned.
▽ ◁ Taking on supplies and ammunition before another cruise.
▽ ▽ ◁ German submariners go through their escape drill while still in training.
▽ A U-boat heads out towards the open sea.
▷ △ A U-boat commander sweeps the horizon through his periscope.
▷ ▽ The constant—and vital—chore on a submerged U-boat: keeping the ship's trim stable.

are finished." In Mordal's opinion, this was a woeful error of judgement, since the horizontal protection to these pens comprised two 12-feet thick layers of concrete, and as the pens themselves were also well-protected with A.A. guns, they stood up to all that the British and American air forces could throw at them.

Britain's losses

From a consideration of Great Britain's defences, let us now look at her losses, especially as we have the memoirs of Admirals Raeder and Dönitz, and also the historical works of Vice-Admiral Assmann and Captain Gerhard Bidlingmaier to help us.

Statistics published after the war, and therefore free of any taint of war-time propaganda, show that the year 1941 cost Allied and neutral shipping 1,299 ships, displacing 4,328,558 tons, an increase of 240 ships and some 340,000 tons over 1940. If we split up these figures according to the way the losses were incurred, we find that losses to submarine action were down slightly, to 2,171,754 tons, as against the 2,186,158 tons of 1940. On the other hand the Luftwaffe considerably increased its total of tonnage destroyed, from 580,074 to over one million, though it has to be remembered that in April and May the evacuation of Greece, and then of Crete, had cost British shipping dear. This makes it easier to understand why, until the Stukas could be eliminated, the British High Command was so reserved in discussing plans for a European second front, which Harry Hopkins and General Marshall had submitted for its consideration, with the enthusiastic backing of President Roosevelt, as early as the spring of 1942.

The tonnage sunk by surface warships, including camouflaged surface raiders, was almost the same for both years, and the menace of the magnetic mine, which made its first appearance in November 1939, was greatly reduced and no longer represented a real threat: 13 per cent of all ships destroyed in 1940, but only $5\frac{1}{2}$ per cent in 1941.

Since Admiral Raeder's staff calculated that British and Canadian shipyards produced 1,600,000 tons annually, Allied shipping thus sustained for 1941 a net loss of 2,700,000 tons, excluding ships that were out of service for repair. However,

the Japanese attack on Pearl Harbor and the declaration of war by Germany and Italy on the U.S.A. on December 11, 1941, placed the enormous resources of the American shipyards, estimated by the Germans at more than 5,000,000 tons for 1942, at the disposal of Great Britain–a major turning-point in the Battle.

The wolf-packs attack

At the beginning of 1942, Admiral Dönitz, from his command post at Kernével near Lorient, had 22 submarines operating under his orders, while another 67, based on Gotenhafen, as the Germans now called Gdynia, were carrying out their trials in the Baltic. For the first two months of the

year, the heavy storms which lashed the North Atlantic severely limited the number of U-boat successes, just as they made it impossible for the British convoy escorts to sink a single submarine. March enabled the two adversaries to resume the struggle in more normal conditions; 41 British and Allied vessels (243,021 tons) were torpedoed and sunk by Dönitz's wolf packs.

This success was, however, dearly bought. Five U-boats were sunk, three of them by the five destroyers and two corvettes which, under the command of Captain Donald Macintyre, were escorting convoy H.X. 112. Besides these, on March 18, *U-47*, commanded by Günther Prien, famous for his Scapa Flow exploit and credited with 28 ships sunk as well as *Royal Oak*, was lost with all hands to an attack by the destroyer *Wolverine*. The first attack on the submerged submarine had bent its propeller shafts. According to Captain Macintyre's account:

"Surfacing after dark in the hope of escaping the destroyer, which had clung persistently to an intermittent asdic contact, the submarine's propellers emitted a rattle clearly to be heard on *Wolverine*'s asdic, leading her accurately to the target. Further depth-charge attacks shattered *U-47*'s hull. A vivid flash and an explosion from the depths told of her end, confirmed as wooden debris floated to the surface."

Disastrous losses

During the night of March 15–16, U-boats succeeded in sinking five of convoy H.X. 112's merchantmen and tankers. But the destroyer *Vanoc*, thanks to her radar, managed to locate, ram, and sink *U-100*, whose captain, Joachim Schepke, was killed in the collision. A particularly aggressive submarine commander, Schepke had been credited with the sinking of 39 ships totalling 159,130 tons. Almost simultaneously, the destroyer *Walker*, under Captain Macintyre, depth-charged *U-99*, which had used all its torpedoes; completely crippled, the German submarine was able to remain on the surface just long enough for its crew to escape. Wearing his officer's peaked cap and with his binoculars slung round his neck – the binoculars had been presented to him by Admiral Dönitz – Otto Kretschmer was the last man to be hoisted aboard *Walker*. With 44 ships totalling 266,629 tons to his credit, Kretschmer was the U-boat "ace of aces", and as such had been decorated with the Oak Leaves to his Knight's Cross of the Iron Cross. He spent the first stage of his captivity in Captain Macintyre's cabin, showing himself to be as redoubtable an opponent at the bridge table as behind his periscope.

May, with 58 ships sunk, a total of 325,492 tons, was the worst month for Great Britain in the Battle of the Atlantic; and if we add to this the losses incurred in the Aegean and Mediterranean Seas during the campaign in the Balkans we find that Allied shipping had lost nearly 1,200,000 tons in two months; Germany was within an ace of the figures Raeder and Dönitz had calculated as being necessary to bring Britain to her knees, without undertaking any other military action.

However, the second half of the year, as a simple comparison with the first half shows, was far from justifying the optimism felt in Dönitz's Kernével H.Q.: between July and December, for various political and strategic reasons, the monthly average of shipping sunk by the U-boats slumped by 50 per cent, to only 120,000 tons.

Firstly, the posting of American naval forces near Greenland and Iceland, and the inclusion of the North Atlantic between Iceland and eastern Newfoundland in the American security zone enabled the British Admiralty to release ships in that area for the strengthening of escorts in the eastern Atlantic. This was especially important; as we have mentioned earlier, Hitler had given strict instructions to avoid any trouble with the U.S.A. The

△ *Dönitz and his staff ponder their next move. Apart from co-ordinating the movements of the U-boats at sea into an overall strategy, Dönitz fought a constant and unsuccessful battle with the Luftwaffe for more long-range patrolling aircraft.*

◁△△ *With the horizon clear, a U-boat pitches to the Atlantic swell, running on the surface on its diesel engines.*

◁△ *Survivors from a sunk merchantman are hauled alongside a U-boat for interrogation, to be given their bearings to the nearest land, and, if necessary, to be given clothing and medical aid.*

◁▽ *A narrow escape. This U-boat is limping back to base after being rammed by an escort vessel during an attack.*

△ △ *Innocent-looking but deadly: one of Germany's fleet of disguised merchant raiders which operated with conspicuous success in 1940 and 1941. This is* Kormoran, *armed with six 5.9-inch guns, four 21-inch torpedo tubes, and carrying two aircraft. She was out for 352 days and sank or captured 11 ships with a total tonnage of 68,264. Her end was a dramatic one: on November 19, 1941, she encountered the Australian cruiser* Sydney *and in a furious battle the two ships sank each other.*

△ *The* Sydney, *last seen as a blazing wreck on the horizon from* Kormoran's *lifeboats. Not a man survived to tell the story of the Australian cruiser's end.*

U-boats had stuck to them, despite the fact that on September 11, 1941 the U.S. Navy ships in the Atlantic had been told to shoot on sight.

Secondly, although the number of submarines operational had increased from 22 in January to 65 in July, and to 91 by the end of the year, not all of them were employed on this vital task of destroying enemy shipping, despite Dönitz's frenzied pleas; with the increase in submarine numbers, Hitler seemed to think he could post them anywhere. Some of his decisions were correct, others much less so.

Thus the beginning of hostilities against the Russians seemed to him to demand the sending of four submarines to the Arctic. Because they found no targets there worthy of their torpedoes, they were recalled, but were not posted back to their essential task, for the Führer had decreed

that Norway constituted a "zone of destiny", and would probably be Churchill's first objective. Dönitz thought such an enterprise out of the question. He was probably right, but it still remains a fact that Churchill gave Sir Alan Brooke, Commander-in-Chief, Home Forces, express instructions to cease all other activity and prepare a plan to attack Trondheim. It was only after a week's polite but steadfast objections that Brooke was able to note in his diary on October 12: "The meeting finished shortly after 8.30 p.m. and for the second time Winston had been ridden off Trondheim." All of which would seem to indicate that, in this case at least, Hitler was right and Dönitz wrong.

Dönitz's forces were further weakened by the continuously worsening situation in the Central Mediterranean. On the orders of O.K.W., six submarines passed through the Straits of Gibraltar at the end of September, being joined in Eleusis harbour by four more in November. In the last chapter we saw the useful contribution they made to the Italians' strategy, just when the southern theatre of operations was being gravely threatened. However, it had been agreed that once their mission had been accomplished, they would return to service in the Atlantic. But this was a meaningless phrase: the current in the middle of the Strait flows very rapidly from the Atlantic to the Mediterranean, which prevented the U-boats from returning underwater, while one night was not long enough to allow them to return on the surface. At the end of December the German Navy had no fewer than 23 U-boats in the Mediterranean, unable to play any part in the battle of the Atlantic (to say nothing of four submarines which had been lost while entering the Mediterranean).

Lastly, expecting an "Anglo-Gaullist" landing in French North Africa, Hitler sent an order to Admiral Dönitz on November 29 to post 15 U-boats on either side of the Strait of Gibraltar. Dönitz thought that the rumours upon which Hitler had based his decision were quite false, but when, at the end of December, Churchill and Roosevelt met in Washington for the "Arcadia" Conference, this was the very plan they agreed on: as soon as Operation "Crusader", then being carried out, had completed the destruction of Axis forces in Cyrenaica, General Auchinleck would implement Operation "Acrobat", bringing the British 8th Army quickly up to the

Returning to this question in the light of the extra information available after the war, Captain S. W. Roskill comes down, with slight reservations, in favour of Dönitz's arguments:

"But the transfer [of U-boats] from the Atlantic brought us a most welcome easement in that vital theatre. The German Staff, when it ordered the U-boats to the Mediterranean, did not know of the Japanese intention to attack on the 7th of December, and could not therefore have foretold that a new ally would assist greatly towards propping up Italy and saving the Axis armies in North Africa. But, in the long view, it may be doubted whether the redistribution of the enemy's U-boat strength brought him any advan-

Tunisian border; after which an expeditionary force, Anglo-American rather than Anglo-Gaullist as first envisaged, would carry out Operation "Gymnast", appearing unexpectedly on the Atlantic coast of Morocco and at suitable points in Algeria and Tunisia. The local French authorities and the Vichy Government would thus be given a last chance to choose between "a blessing or a cursing", as Churchill put it in a note of December 16. We know what happened to this plan, but it is clear that Hitler was right to be concerned about such an eventuality, and about the means of countering it.

On December 31, therefore, there were 91 U-boats available, split up as follows:

Mediterranean	26
West of Gibraltar	6
Norway	4
Available to Dönitz	55

tage, because of the decline in his Atlantic offensive which it made inevitable."

With 55 U-boats at his disposal for the blockade of Britain, Dönitz would have done much better if he had been able to use them in co-operation with air and surface forces. He could of course rely on Lieutenant-Colonel Martin Harlinghausen, commanding *Kampfgeschwader 40* at Bordeaux, equipped with Focke-Wulf 200 Condors, adequate maritime reconnaissance/bomber machines. But the immense enthusiasm and intelligence of this former naval officer could not compensate for the very limited serviceability rate of his unit's aircraft – only two per day at the most, instead of the 12 that Dönitz would have liked. And yet, each time that aircraft and U-boats were able to co-operate, the results proved most encouraging, and this tiny handful of four-engined German

△ The Gneisenau *copes easily with the Atlantic swell during her successful raiding cruise with* Scharnhorst. *Both ships were launched at the end of 1936 and worked as an efficient team, sinking between them 115,622 tons of shipping. It was the success of this operation that prompted the Germans to launch* Bismarck *and the* Prinz Eugen *on Operation "Rheinübung". The new operation would bring all four ships together to harass the Atlantic sealanes.*

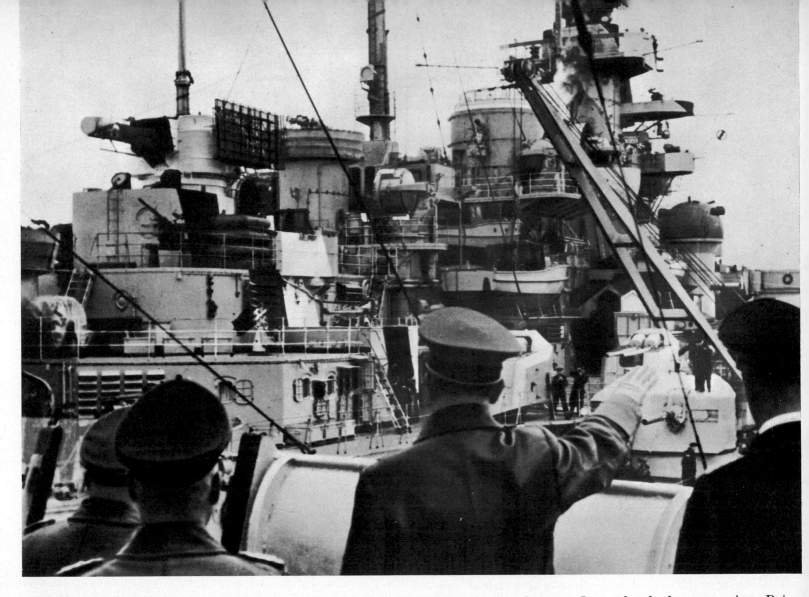

bombers produced considerable consternation among Allied convoys.

With a little more diplomacy, would Dönitz have been able to bring home to the vindictive and presumptuous Hermann Göring a more accurate realisation of what was really needed for naval and air forces to co-operate successfully? This is most unlikely because, on Hitler's express instructions, Göring combined responsibility for the Wehrmacht's air operations with the industrial dictatorship of the Third Reich and the occupied countries, and flitted from one sphere of activity to the other with the most disconcerting frivolity, apparently quite incapable of setting his mind to a problem and carrying it through to a reasonable conclusion.

Another factor militating against the effective waging of the battle of the Atlantic was the pitifully small number of maintenance personnel available to Dönitz. And even these could not do all that they might have done as a result of several unforeseeable circumstances.

On March 23, 1941, at the end of a lightning raid, the battle-cruisers *Scharnhorst* and *Gneisenau* put in at Brest, being joined

there on June 1 by the heavy cruiser *Prinz Eugen*, which had succeeded, in circumstances related below, in escaping from the battle which had resulted in the sinking of *Bismarck*. The concentration of three such powerful units in one place provoked a violent reaction from the R.A.F.

On April 6, an R.A.F. pilot succeeded in hitting *Gneisenau* with a torpedo, and after she had been towed back to harbour, she was hit again, this time by four bombs. On July 1 a British bomber hit *Prinz Eugen*, putting her out of commission for four months. Lastly, *Scharnhorst* was hit by five bombs while on trials off la Pallice.

In order to repair these surface warships as soon as possible, maintenance crews despite Dönitz's strongest protests, were taken off submarine work in considerable numbers, and the overhaul and repair of U-boats consequently suffered.

Thus, at the end of the year, 60 per cent of Dönitz's U-boats were out of action, and of the 22 left, ten were in transit, leaving only 12 for operations over the whole theatre of operations from Cape Farewell in Greenland to the Azores.

Meanwhile, Admiral Sir Percy Noble'

anti-submarine forces had increased both in quantity and quality. This is clearly shown by the results of the battle, from Gibraltar to Ushant, between U-boats and the escort for the 32 merchantmen of convoy H.G. 76 between December 14–23. The British Admiralty had gone to great lengths to protect this convoy, giving Captain F. J. Walker, commanding the escort force, an escort carrier, three destroyers, four sloops, and no fewer than ten corvettes.

After nine days of relentless combat, the losses were these:
1. Britain: escort carrier *Audacity*, lost to *U-751* (Lieutenant Bigalk) and destroyer *Stanley*;
2. Germany: two Focke-Wulf Condors, shot down by *Audacity*'s fighters, and five of the ten submarines involved. One of these was *U-567*, commanded by Lieutenant Endrass, whose total tonnage sunk was very close to the record set shortly before by Otto Kretschmer.

In short, the British had had the best of the engagement, especially as 30 of the 32 merchantmen reached their destination.

1941 had cost the Germans 35 U-boats, of which three had been lost in the Baltic and five in the Mediterranean. During the first half of the year, however, the shipyards of the Reich had been producing new U-boats at the rate of 13 a month, a figure that increased to 20 in the second half of the year. Thus the U-boat arm gained a total of 163 boats during the year (a production of 198 minus 35 boats lost). Dönitz therefore had no reason to be pessimistic, especially as the German and Italian declarations of war on the United States on December 11, 1941 left his boats free to attack American shipping. To complete the picture, it should be noted that the Italians lost eight boats in the battle of the Atlantic.

During the same period, Germany's surface warships destroyed 427,000 tons of Allied shipping, slightly less than one-fifth of the tonnage despatched by the U-boats. By this activity, however, the surface raiders tied down ships that could profitably have been used elsewhere. Battleships, for example, had to be escorted by four destroyers, and this weakening of the anti-submarine effort made Dönitz's task that much easier.

On January 1, 1941, there were six German disguised surface raiders (con-

verted cargo or banana boats) at large on the high seas: two in the Pacific, two in the Indian Ocean, and two in the South Atlantic. Operating either singly or in pairs, they scuttled their prey after taking off supplies for their own use or sent them off with a skeleton crew to one of the French Atlantic ports if their cargoes of food or industrial supplies could be of use to the Reich.

There were, for example, three Norwegian whaling factory ships captured by *Pinguin* off the Antarctic ice-pack on January 14–15. Slipping through the British patrols, they managed to reach Bordeaux. *Pinguin* had left Germany on June 22, 1940 and had sunk 28 merchantmen (137,000 tons) when she was surprised and sunk by the cruiser *Cornwall* on May 8, 1941, off Somaliland.

On November 19, 1941, another German raider, *Kormoran*, was sunk off the coast of Western Australia by the cruiser *Sydney*. But before going down with most of her crew, she torpedoed her attacker, which sank with all hands. *Kormoran* had been at sea for more than ten months and had 11 ships (68,000 tons) to her credit.

Three days later Germany lost a further raider. *Atlantis* was caught while transferring supplies to a U-boat half way between Guinea and Brazil. She was sunk quickly by the 8-inch guns of the cruiser *Devonshire* after a cruise that had brought her 22 victims (146,000 tons) in 1½ years.

The three remaining raiders, *Komet, Thor,* and *Orion,* were luckier, and managed to get back to Germany under the very noses of the Allies. The most noteworthy of their cruises was probably that of *Komet,* commanded by Captain Eyssen, who was promoted to Rear-Admiral on the last day of 1940. *Komet* left Hamburg on June 6, 1940 and returned there on April 30, 1941, after cruising right round the world. With the aid of Russian icebreakers she had made the North-East Passage, skirted Siberia, and entered the Pacific via the Bering Strait. After taking her toll of Allied shipping in the Pacific in conjunction with *Orion,* she returned to Hamburg via the Cape of Good Hope, her whole cruise having taken her something like 100,000 miles.

From figures released after the war, it seems that *Komet, Thor,* and *Orion* accounted for 33 merchantmen totalling about 183,000 tons. In addition to these, *Thor* met and sank the British auxiliary cruiser *Voltaire* on April 4, 1941, picking up 196 survivors.

△ *Captain Bernhard Rogge of the* Atlantis, *the "top-scoring" disguised merchant raider commander with 22 ships.*

△ *Captain Otto Kähler of the* Thor. *He fought three extremely punishing battles against British auxiliary cruisers –* Alcantara, Carnarvon Castle, *and* Voltaire.
▽ *Captain Helmuth von Rückteschell of the* Widder.

The British battle-cruiser *Hood*

Displacement: 42,100 tons.
Armament: eight 15-inch, twelve 5.5-inch, eight 4-inch A.A., twenty-four 2-pdr A.A., and twenty .5-inch guns, and four 21-inch torpedo tubes.
Armour: 5- to 12-inch belt, $1\frac{1}{4}$- to $3\frac{3}{4}$-inch deck, 11- to 15-inch turrets, and 9- to 11-inch control tower.
Speed: 31 knots.
Length: $860\frac{1}{2}$ feet.
Beam: $105\frac{1}{4}$ feet.
Draught: $28\frac{1}{2}$ feet.
Complement: 1,341.

The German battleship *Bismarck*

Displacement: 41,700 tons.
Armament: eight 15-inch, twelve 5.9-inch, sixteen 4.1-inch A.A., sixteen 3.7-cm A.A., and twelve 2-cm A.A. guns, eight 21-inch torpedo tubes, and six aircraft.
Armour: 12.6-inch belt, 8-inch deck, and 14-inch turrets.
Speed: 30 knots.
Radius: 8,100 miles at 19 knots.
Length: 792 feet.
Beam: 118 feet.
Draught: 26 feet.
Complement: 2,400.

CHAPTER 55
Bismarck's agony

△ Bismarck *and* Prinz Eugen, *grim in their dazzle camouflage, lie at anchor in Korsfjord before making their dramatic break-out into the North Atlantic through the Denmark Strait.*

At the beginning of 1941, the pocket-battleship *Admiral Scheer*, a sister ship of the ill-fated *Graf Spee*, was operating in the South Atlantic in collaboration with *Pinguin,* which *Scheer* provided with the crews necessary to sail back to France the three factory ships mentioned above. On February 2 she sailed round the Cape of Good Hope and made contact with *Atlantis.* The two German vessels then operated together in the Moçambique Channel. Among their victims was the tanker *British Advocate,* whose cargo was naturally enough greatly prized by the two raiders.

On March 6, having sunk or captured 16 ships (99,000 tons) *Admiral Scheer* began her voyage home. She slipped past the two British cruisers on watch in the Denmark Strait. On April 1 she docked at Kiel, after 161 days at sea. During her cruise, *Admiral Scheer* had covered over 50,000 miles, a tribute indeed to her robust diesel engines and the magnificent spirit that Captain Krancke had instilled into his crew.

A month and a half earlier, the heavy cruiser *Admiral Hipper*, commanded by Captain Meisel, had also reached Kiel. She had sailed from Brest on February 1, and on the 12th intercepted a convoy from Gibraltar between the Azores and Madeira. In less than 90 minutes she sank seven merchantmen (33,000 tons) with her 8-inch guns and with torpedoes.

The return of these two warships was

facilitated by Operation "Berlin"–the attacks carried out against British shipping in the North Atlantic by the battle-cruisers *Scharnhorst* and *Gneisenau.* Under the command of Admiral Günther Lütjens, the *Flottenchef* or Fleet Commander, the two battle-cruisers had sailed from Kiel on January 23 and passed through the Denmark Strait, after a few anxious moments, on the night of February 3. But their mission was dogged by crippling restrictions. Raeder had told Lütjens: "the essential task of the squadron is to be the destruction of enemy shipping . . . In the course of its attacks on enemy shipping it is on no account to engage an enemy of equal strength . . . it is also to avoid an engagement even if it encounters a single battle-cruiser armed with 15-inch guns."

On February 8, the German force spotted convoy H.X. 106, which had sailed from Halifax for Great Britain on January 31. The convoy was escorted by the old battle-

ship *Ramillies,* however, and in accordance with his orders Lütjens broke off contact, despite the fact that the captain of *Scharnhorst* had offered to draw off the escort and thus give *Gneisenau* the opportunity to annihilate the convoy. The plan entailed little risk as *Scharnhorst* was a good 11 knots faster than *Ramillies,* but Lütjens stuck rigidly to his orders.

A fortnight later, off Newfoundland, the German squadron sank three cargo vessels and two tankers of an America-bound convoy that had scattered on being attacked. Then, heading south-east, the German ships found themselves on March 3 less than 300 miles from Tenerife in the Canary islands, well-placed to attack convoys on the Gibraltar–Freetown run. On the morning of the 8th, a dozen merchantmen came over the horizon, escorted, however, by the battleship *Malaya,* armed, like *Ramillies,* with 15-inch guns. Still obeying orders, Lütjens stood off, though he did try to direct towards the convoy the two

△ *What Raeder hoped would be repeated with* Rheinübung, *the war cruise of* Bismarck: *a defenceless merchantman is shelled by the 4.1-inch secondary armament of* Hipper, *which sank seven ships sailing in an unescorted convoy in February 1941.*

U-boats operating in the area–no easy task, as German surface vessels and U-boats did not use the same code, and it was only by the roundabout route Paris–Kernével that he was able to pass on the information.

Then *Scharnhorst* and *Gneisenau*, accompanied by their two supply ships, moved off north-west again to intercept the Halifax–Great Britain route. Here they managed to avoid the attentions of the battleship *Nelson* while sinking or capturing 16 ships on March 15–16.

"As day broke on March 16," write J. Vulliez and J. Mordal, "the squadron was surrounded by merchantmen which, seeing the Germans, scattered in all directions. The hunt began with *Ermland* forcing a large cargo vessel within range of *Scharnhorst*, whose guns quickly sank her. Immediately afterwards *Gneisenau* sank an unidentified ship of 5,000 tons at long range. And so the hunt went on: while *Scharnhorst* was sinking the 4,350-ton *Silverfix*, *Uckermark* forced five ships within range of *Gneisenau*, which picked them off one by one. Time was running out, and it was getting too late for the attackers to think of making any captures. At about 1500, just when the chase seemed over, the two battle-cruisers increased speed and caught one more merchantman."

It was about this time that Lütjens received orders to create a diversion, to enable *Admiral Hipper* and *Admiral Scheer* to slip through the Denmark Strait. With the choice of heading for the Azores or Brest, Lütjens chose the latter. He passed through the dangerous Iroise between the islands of Ushant and Sein at 0700 in March 22.

Dr. Goebbels' propaganda machine made great play with the warships' safe return, heaping scorn on the Royal Navy which, in spite of its overwhelming numer-ical superiority, had not even been able to engage the two German ships, let alone sink them. In reality, the situation was rather different and in no way justified such jubilation.

While it was true that the two raiders had sunk 22 merchantmen, totalling 116,000 tons, this very creditable result had its gloomy side in the disastrous state of their engines after two months' continuous cruising. And since the same comments were made about *Admiral Hipper*, one can only conclude that high-pressure turbine engines were the weak link in German marine engineering.

At all events, repairs to *Gneisenau's* engines took several weeks, and to *Scharnhorst's* even longer. It therefore became clear that neither could participate in Operation *"Rheinübung"*, which was to have consisted in a raid on British shipping by *Bismarck* and the heavy cruiser *Prinz Eugen*, combined with a further sortie by the two battle-cruisers.

Operation *"Rheinübung"*

Although a great deal has been written in Great Britain and Germany about the four days which sealed the fates of the two giant warships *Hood* and *Bismarck*, together with most of their crews, the full circumstances of this tragic episode are still not clear. More than a quarter of a century later, the reasons for certain decisions remain wrapped in mystery; Admirals Holland and Lütjens have taken their secrets with them to the grave, and the survivors of the two ships (three from *Hood* and 115 from *Bismarck*), included only four junior officers (one British and three German), who could not give the reasons for their superiors' decisions.

What we do know is that the objective

and execution of Operation *"Rheinübung"* were first described in a directive from Grand-Admiral Raeder on April 2, 1941.

In contrast with the orders given to *Scharnhorst* and *Gneisenau, Bismarck*'s squadron would this time be allowed to attack escorted convoys, but *Bismarck* herself could take on an opponent of equal strength only to allow other members of the squadron to get at the merchantmen. "The essential objective," said Raeder in section four of his directive, "remains the destruction of enemy shipping. An attack on an enemy warship can take place only

Originally intended to displace 35,000 tons, *Bismarck* in fact displaced 41,700 tons when ready for service. She had been commissioned on August 24, 1940, and so as she made ready for her first and last sortie, had nine months of intensive training behind her. During this time, Captain Lindemann had brought both ship and crew to a high level of efficiency.

Prinz Eugen, commanded by Captain Brinkmann, was another brand new ship. Displacing 13,900 tons, she was armed with eight 8-inch guns in four two-gun turrets, twelve 4.1-inch A.A. guns, twelve

insofar as the success of the mission warrants it, and even then excessive risks are to be avoided."

Raeder's increased aggressiveness was justified by *Bismarck*'s powerful offensive armament and superb defensive strength. The battleship's main armament consisted of eight 15-inch guns in four two-gun turrets and, beside the superb optical ranging equipment possessed by German warships, *Bismarck* was fitted with a "radiotelemeter", a 90-cm wavelength type of radar, for range calculating. The battleship's secondary armament consisted of twelve 5.9-inch, sixteen 4.1-inch A.A., and sixteen 3.7-cm A.A. guns. Defensively, she had a 12.6-inch belt of armour on the hull, turrets armoured to 14-inches thickness and decks 8 inches thick. Her great beam (118 feet) and large number of watertight compartments gave her a high degree of underwater protection, and her engines, developing 138,000-hp, enabled her to reach 30 knots.

3.7-cm A.A. guns, and twelve 21-inch torpedo tubes. Her engines, which seem to have been more reliable than those of her sister ship *Admiral Hipper,* gave her a top speed of 32 knots. On April 23, however, she struck a mine in the Baltic, and *"Rheinübung"* had to be put off till May.

Since *Scharnhorst* and *Gneisenau* were undergoing repairs, they were unable to carry out the diversions assigned to them, and Admiral Lütjens expressed the opinion that it would be better if the operation were postponed until the two battle-cruisers were once again ready for sea. He even went so far as to suggest that *Tirpitz, Bismarck*'s sister ship, should be commissioned first. The objection to that, however, was that the surface fleet would thus have been condemned to long weeks of inactivity. Raeder would have none of it, so Lütjens withdrew his objections.

On the evening of May 20, after passing through the Kattegat, *Bismarck* and *Prinz Eugen* emerged into the North Sea.

△ Bismarck *under way in the Baltic, seen from* Prinz Eugen. *The two ships sailed from Gdynia (Gotenhafen) on May 18 and passed through the Great Belt and the Kattegat into the North Sea on May 20. Their first objective was Norway, where they topped up with fuel and made the final preparations for the crucial break-out into the Atlantic.*

The nearest Home Fleet
warship with the most chances
of tackling Bismarck on equal
terms was the pride of the Royal
Navy: the legendary battle-
cruiser Hood, for years the
ultimate expression of Britain's
naval strength.
▷ The boast which Hood upheld
for 20 years, in ventures like the
famous Empire round-the-world
cruise in the 1920's and off the
coast of Spain during the
Civil War.
▽ The clean, elegant lines of
Hood, shown to perfection as she
lies at anchor in Scapa Flow.
Her main trouble when pitted
against Bismarck was not her
age but her design. She was a
battle-cruiser, not a battleship:
longer and leaner, with the same
broadside of eight 15-inch guns
as the German battleship, but
with less emphasis on armoured
protection. Her real tragedy was
that when war came in 1939 she
was scheduled for a complete
refit which would have
transformed her into a much
tougher and more hard-hitting
battleship.

The news leaks out

As early as the following morning, news
that the two German warships had left
the Baltic reached London. The Admiralty
immediately alerted Admiral Sir John
Tovey, C.-in-C. Home Fleet, and also
informed him that the aircraft-carrier
Victorious and battle-cruiser *Repulse* had
been put at his disposal. Reconnaissance
photographs taken the next day identified
Bismarck and an *Admiral Hipper*-class
heavy cruiser in Korsfjord, south of
Bergen.

Without dismissing entirely such ex-
planations for *Bismarck*'s move as an
invasion of Iceland, Tovey was fairly sure
that the real reason was a second German
naval sortie into the Atlantic. Consequently he strengthened the patrols along
the Orkneys–Shetlands–Faeroes–Iceland–Greenland line, and on the evening
of May 21 ordered Vice-Admiral L. E.
Holland's Battle-Cruiser Squadron (the
battle-cruiser *Hood*, battleship *Prince of*

Wales, and six destroyers) to sail from Scapa Flow to Hvalfjord. Tovey would thus be assured of a considerable superiority in fire-power over his adversary: eight 15-inch and ten 14-inch guns against eight 15-inch guns.

It is true, however, that *Hood*, for all her 42,100 tons displacement and 860-foot length, was beginning to show her age. Commissioned in 1920, she reflected World War I ideas of naval warfare. In particular her defences against plunging fire left a great deal to be desired. *Hood*'s companion capital ship in the squadron, *Prince of Wales* was fitted with a main armament of a calibre new to the Royal Navy, and had not yet proved herself. Two of her three gun turrets (one two-gun and two four-gun) had only been fitted on April 28. Indeed, when she weighed anchor, there were still workmen on board trying to iron out her teething troubles, and these civilians went to sea with her.

On May 22 another reconnaissance of Korsfjord made in abominable weather, showed that the two German ships had gone, so at 2245 the main fleet sailed from Scapa Flow under Admiral Tovey. Beside *King George V*, a sister ship of *Prince of Wales*, Tovey also had the aircraft-carrier *Victorious*, four cruisers, and seven destroyers. The battle-cruiser *Repulse*, coming from the Clyde, joined him later. Operation *"Rheinübung"* was under way.

Admiral Lütjens had a choice of two passages through which to break out into the Atlantic: the Denmark Strait between Iceland and Greenland, which had been reduced to 60 miles in width by a minefield and pack ice, and the 300-mile wide gap between the Faeroes and Iceland. His staff advised him to choose the latter, but he opted for the former, as he knew it from an earlier sortie. Captain Bidlingmaier considers this choice to have been mistaken, pointing out that had they taken the route south of Iceland, the German ships could have slipped through the area between the Battle-Cruiser Squadron and the Home Fleet. As the British had only three cruisers on patrol in the area, Bidlingmaier is surely correct.

First contact

Perhaps the German admiral had reckoned on fog and rain to hide his movements; but if he did, he had reckoned without radar.

On May 23, at 1922, the cruiser *Suffolk* spotted *Bismarck* and her companion. She then dodged into a patch of mist to prevent *Bismarck* from firing on her, and sent out a report of the German ships' position, while shadowing them by radar. About an hour later *Suffolk* was joined by her sister ship *Norfolk* (Rear-Admiral W. F. Wake-Walker), which made the first enemy report received by Tovey. The two cruisers then shadowed the German squadron by radar.

At 0535 the following morning, using the information so ably provided by *Suffolk* and *Norfolk*, the Battle-Cruiser Squadron sighted *Bismarck* and *Prinz Eugen* off the starboard bow, in an excellent position in which they could be fired on by all turrets. Yet a few minutes later Vice-Admiral Holland altered course, with the result that the rear turrets of his ships could no longer bear: the British superiority in firepower which, as we have seen, was in the order of 18 to 8, had thus been reduced to 10 to 8, and after the first salvo 9 to 8, as one of *Prince of Wales*'s 14-inch guns could not be reloaded.

Holland's manoeuvre has given rise to a great deal of controversy, and many critics have taken him severely to task for going into battle with one hand tied behind his back, so to speak. Roskill, however, impartial as always, has pointed out that ballistic considerations may have dictated the change of course. For beyond a range of about 12,000 yards, the German shells, plunging down at a steep angle, would have torn straight through *Hood*'s inadequately armoured deck. By making directly for his enemy, Holland could get his ship inside the dangerous plunging trajectory of *Bismarck*'s shells to a position where any hits would be on the 12-inch belt rather than $3\frac{3}{4}$-inch deck.

The death of the *Hood*

At all events, at 0552 Admiral Holland gave the order to open fire, concentrating on the leading German ship. During the night, however, *Prinz Eugen* and *Bismarck* had changed places, with the result that the fire of *Hood* was now directed against the former. *Bismarck* was correctly identified by *Prince of Wales*, which thus fired on the second ship. But this meant that the anticipated superiority in guns of 18 to 8 had now become an inferiority of 5 to 8.

Admiral Sir John Tovey, the C.-in-C., Home Fleet, from 1940 to 1943, was the man on whom Britain depended to counter any sorties by the small but formidable German battle fleet. His constant dilemma was to apportion sufficient protection to the Atlantic convoys while retaining a large enough concentration of heavy warships to cope with any break-out by German capital ships. His greatest achievement was his handling of the *Bismarck* episode—the biggest job yet tackled by the Home Fleet.

Vice-Admiral L. E. Holland commanded the Home Fleet's Battle-Cruiser Squadron. His was an unenviable command, for *Prince of Wales* had been rushed into service so rapidly that not all her guns were fully operational. His decision to close the range as fast as possible before opening full broadsides gave the Germans a decided superiority in firepower when the shooting started.

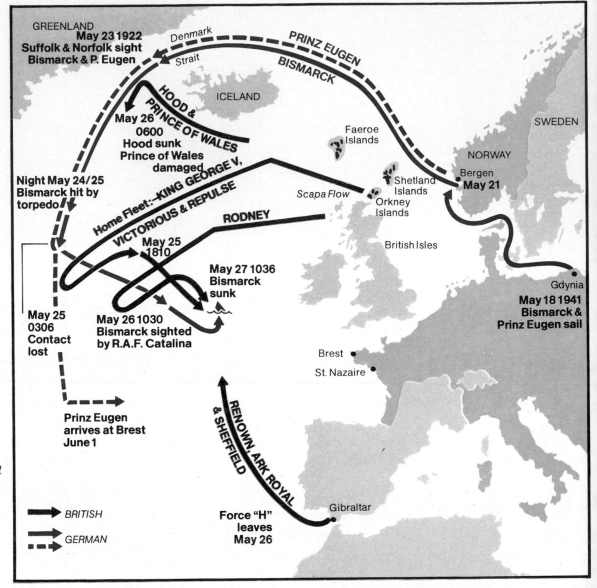

GREENLAND
May 23 1922
Suffolk & Norfolk sight
Bismarck & P. Eugen

Denmark
Strait

PRINZ EUGEN
BISMARCK

ICELAND

HOOD & PRINCE OF WALES

May 26
0600
Hood sunk
Prince of Wales
damaged

Night May 24/25
Bismarck hit by
torpedo

Home Fleet:—**KING GEORGE V,**
VICTORIOUS & REPULSE

RODNEY

May 25
1810

May 27 1036
Bismarck
sunk

May 25
0306
Contact
lost

May 26 1030
Bismarck sighted
by R.A.F. Catalina

Faeroe
Islands

Shetland
Islands

Scapa Flow

Orkney
Islands

British Isles

NORWAY
Bergen
May 21

SWEDEN

Gdynia

May 18 1941
Bismarck &
Prinz Eugen sail

Brest
St. Nazaire

Prinz Eugen
arrives at Brest
June 1

RENOWN, ARK ROYAL
& SHEFFIELD

→ BRITISH
⇢ GERMAN

Force "H"
leaves
May 26

Gibraltar

▷ *The epic chase of* Bismarck
was the greatest air-sea pursuit
in the history of naval warfare,
covering the entire North
Atlantic. The widely scattered
British naval dispositions were
converted into a net which closed
in on the track of Bismarck.
Prinz Eugen, *detached by*
Lütjens after the sinking of
Hood, *never even began her*
scheduled programme of
commerce raiding, but ran for
Brest as soon as Bismarck*'s*
pursuers had dispersed.

The crisis of the battle occurred at 0600. Just as the British squadron began to turn to port, in order to bring their after turrets to bear, and with *Hood* about to open fire on *Bismarck*, a 15-inch salvo landed on the British battle-cruiser. Lieutenant-Commander Jaspers, *Prinz Eugen's* gunnery officer, describes the scene thus:

"As a whole salvo of 15-inch shells from the German flagship reached its target, there was an explosion of quite incredible violence, between the second funnel and the mainmast. The salvo seemed to crush everything under it with irresistible force. Through huge holes opened up in the grey hull, enormous flames leapt up from the depths of the ship, far above the funnels, and blazed for several seconds through an ash-coloured pall of smoke, which spread terrifyingly towards the ship's bows. And this grey mass fringed with red, composed of smoke, fire, and steam, was seen to form two billowing columns spreading upwards and outwards, while just below them formed a kind of incandescent dome, whose initial low flat curve rose higher and higher, finally culminating in an explosion of burning debris. The aft magazine blew up, shooting into the air a molten mass the colour of red lead, which then fell back lazily into the sea—it was one of the rear gun turrets that we thus saw rising into the air for several yards. All the inflammable objects in the area at the time—rafts, boats, and deck planking—broke loose, and even as they drifted continued to burn, drawing a thick cloud of smoke over the sea's surface.

"And in the midst of this raging inferno, a yellow tongue of flame shot out just once more: the forward turrets of *Hood* had fired one last salvo."

In the circumstances, it is not surprising that out of a total complement of 95 officers and 1,324 men, there should be only three survivors, the senior being Midshipman W. J. Dundas.

Having disposed of *Hood, Bismarck* and *Prinz Eugen* turned their attention on *Prince of Wales*, which had as yet not been fired on. In the space of only a few minutes, the German ships landed four 15-inch and three 8-inch shells on the British battleship. One shell hit the compass platform, killing or wounding everyone on it except the ship's captain, Captain Leach, and a signaller. *Prince of Wales*'s plight was increased by the fact that breakdown followed breakdown in the turrets. As a result, Captain Leach broke off the engagement under a smoke screen at 0613 and retired.

Having fired only 93 15-inch shells – less than ten per cent of her stock of main-calibre shells – *Bismarck* had obviously achieved brilliant results. But she had also been hit by two of *Prince of Wales*'s 14-inch shells. Considering the teething troubles of her main armament, *Prince of Wales* may be said to have performed very creditably. More important, one of the British shells had hit a fuel bunker, causing it to leak. This contaminated the fuel with sea water, seriously affecting *Bismarck*'s performance, and also caused an enormous ribbon of fuel to trail out behind her. At 0801, therefore, Admiral Lütjens informed his superiors that he intended to make for Saint Nazaire. *Prinz Eugen* had escaped from the clash unscathed, despite several near misses, and later carried out her original orders for operations in the Atlantic.

Admiral Lütjens' decision was discussed at the Berghof by Hitler and Grand-Admiral Raeder on June 6. The Führer was puzzled by two decisions in particular. Firstly, why had Lütjens not returned to a German port after the engagement with *Hood*, and secondly, why had he not pressed home the attack on *Prince of Wales* and destroyed her? Even if the latter had led to the loss of *Bismarck*, the net result would have been the destruction of two British capital ships for one German.

Raeder's answer was, to say the least of things, tortuous. If *Bismarck* had tried to return via the Denmark Strait, as her captain had vainly suggested to Lütjens, nothing would have prevented her safe

At battle stations with the Royal Navy.
▽ *Loading a 4-inch gun–for many light escorts in the Battle of the Atlantic the heaviest gun carried for surface action.*
▽▽ *Anti-aircraft vigil: the crew of a 2-pounder "pom-pom" (these guns were also known as "Chicago pianos" because of their distinctive sound).*

△ *Swordfish torpedo-bombers on the flight-deck of the aircraft-carrier* Victorious – *another Home Fleet capital ship which was brand new and not fully trained. Yet it was from this flight-deck that British aircraft took off for the first time in history to launch a carrier strike against a German battleship at sea. No damage was done by the solitary hit scored on* Bismarck's *armoured belt but it was nevertheless a gallant effort, deserving of better success.*

return to Korsfjord, so far as one can see. This would have meant abandoning her original mission, but this would probably have been inevitable had she tried to finish off *Prince of Wales*, since "she would have been very much the worse for wear, even if she had come off best," as Raeder put it, "and this would certainly have prevented her from continuing her attack on merchant shipping. Her mission compelled her to stand and fight only if the enemy stopped her attacking such shipping."

It is clear that Raeder was using his knowledge and authority to shield his hapless subordinate. All the same, he may have been right, as chance rather than planning played a large part in the ensuing catastrophe.

The Admiralty stunned

Vice-Admiral Wake-Walker's message that *Hood* had blown up, followed by the co-ordinates, was a real bombshell both for *King George V*, then about 450 miles south-east of the position radioed, and for the Admiralty.

But by mid-day, Sir Dudley Pound and his deputy, Vice-Admiral Sir Tom Phillips, had embarked on a whole series of measures designed to remedy the situation and restore the prestige of the Royal Navy. To quote but one example, they had set on *Bismarck's* tail two battle-

ships, one battle-cruiser, one aircraft-carrier, three cruisers, and nine destroyers, not hesitating to rob Atlantic convoys of their escorts in the process. Thus new orders were received by Force H, which had sailed from Gibraltar at 0200 on May 24, and *Rodney*, which was escorting, with four destroyers, the liner *Britannic* to New York.

Off the eastern coast of Greenland, Wake-Walker had taken under his command *Prince of Wales* and the destroyers of the Battle-Cruiser Squadron, and continued to shadow *Bismarck* by radar. Since Lütjens was steering south-west, Tovey closed on an interception course that would allow him to engage the two German ships at some time the following morning, even if they tried to return to the North Sea by passing south of Iceland or to put in at a French port, because of the oil leak, rather than pursue their original plan of hunting down Atlantic merchant shipping. To slow down his opponent, Tovey decided to send in the Swordfish from *Victorious*.

But both *Victorious* and her aircrew were as untried as *Prince of Wales* and, more important, the weather had turned foul. Despite the weather, however, Lieutenant-Commander Esmonde led his Swordfish on an attack on *Bismarck*, he himself landing a hit on the German battleship's armour belt. Unfortunately for the British, this torpedo hit did little but damage the paintwork. In the depth of night all the attacking aircraft managed to relocate *Victorious* and land safely, much to the relief of the aircraft-carrier's captain, Captain H. C. Bovell.

Meanwhile, events had been moving swiftly. First of all Lütjens ordered *Prinz Eugen* to leave *Bismarck* and operate independently, and then, much to Tovey's consternation, *Suffolk* lost contact with *Bismarck*. Matters were not improved by the fact that a long radio message sent by Lütjens at 0400 on May 25 was intercepted by the British. But its bearing was incorrectly plotted and led Tovey to believe that the Germans were attempting to move back into the North Sea. Another serious problem for the British was the fact that hardly an hour passed without one of the Royal Navy's vessels having to withdraw to refuel, some to Iceland, some to Newfoundland, and some even to Gibraltar. In fact, of the 15 units which had sailed on May 22, *King George V* was the only one left in the central Atlantic.

On May 26, however, a patrolling Catalina of Coastal Command spotted *Bismarck*, heading south-east, about 690 miles from Brest:

"'George' (the automatic pilot) was flying the aircraft," said the pilot, "at 500 feet when we saw a warship. I was in the second pilot's seat when the occupant of the seat beside me, an American, said: 'What the devil's that?' I stared and saw a dull black shape through the mist which curled above a very rough sea. 'Looks like a battleship,' he said. I said: 'Better get closer, go round its stern.' I thought it might be the *Bismarck*, because I could see no destroyers round the ship and I should have seen them had she been a British warship. I left my seat, went to the wireless operator's table, grabbed a piece of paper and began to write out a signal."

It was now 1030, and though Admiral Tovey, as a result of the plotting error of the night before, was not in a position to intercept, Sir John Somerville, commander of Force H, was able to send in a strike of Swordfish torpedo-bombers from *Ark Royal*. If they could only succeed in slowing down *Bismarck* before midnight, the battle would be won; otherwise, *King George V* and *Rodney* would be forced to turn back for lack of fuel.

The first strike was launched in squally showers at 1450, but was a total failure. The Swordfish mistakenly attacked the cruiser *Sheffield*, which Admiral Somerville had sent on ahead to keep tabs on *Bismarck*. Fortunately for *Sheffield*, the attack achieved nothing apart from an-other demonstration of British torpedoes' inefficiency: the Fleet Air Arm pilots saw their weapons, fitted with magnetic detonators, exploding as soon as they touched the water. The second strike flew off at 1910, armed with torpedoes fitted with contact pistols and set to run at a shallower depth.

As the 15 aircraft took off, they were observed by Lieutenant-Commander Wolfahrt of *U-556*. In his log he wrote:

"1908 hours: Alert. A battleship of the *King George V*-class and an aircraft-carrier, probably *Ark Royal*, are coming up astern, travelling at great speed. Deflection 10 degrees right. If only I had torpedoes! I am in the perfect position to attack–no need even to manoeuvre. No destroyers, no zig-zags! I could slip between them and fire on both simultaneously. Torpedo planes are taking off from the aircraft-carrier. Perhaps I could have helped *Bismarck*."

▽ *The gunner of a Swordfish checks out his .303-inch machine gun. The Swordfish of the veteran* Ark Royal, *which joined in the hunt for* Bismarck *from Gibraltar, launched the torpedo which jammed the German battleship's rudder and made it possible for Tovey's battleships to intercept. Conditions were so bad, however, that* Ark Royal's *Swordfish managed to attack the British cruiser* Sheffield *in error. "Sorry for the kippers," they signalled to* Sheffield *as they returned to* Ark Royal *to rearm for the decisive strike.*

Apart from the error of identifying *Renown* for a *King George V*-class battleship, there is no reason to doubt the validity of Wolfahrt's narrative.

Bismarck sunk

Despite a hail of fire from all *Bismarck*'s guns, the Swordfish strike went in successfully between 2047 and 2125 and scored two hits. The first struck *Bismarck*'s armour belt and caused no damage, but the second hit aft, damaging her propellers, wrecking her steering gear, and jamming her rudders. After desperate but unsuccessful efforts to free them, Lütjens sent the following message: "No longer able to steer ship. Will fight to last shell. Long live the Führer."

After describing two complete circles, the luckless *Bismarck* headed slowly

north-north-west, straight towards *King George V* and *Rodney*. But before she met these two battleships, she ran into five destroyers led by Captain Vian, which had been taken off convoy duty to act as an anti-submarine screen for Sir John Tovey's main fleet. Seeing *Bismarck's* drastically reduced speed, Vian decided to attack. So heavy was the sea running, and so accurate *Bismarck's* fire, that of the 16 torpedoes fired by the one Polish and four British destroyers, possibly only two of them struck home.

The following morning, *King George V* and *Rodney*, guided by *Norfolk*, arrived on the scene. The two battleships opened fire on *Bismarck*, which was moving at seven knots, at 0847 and 0848 respectively, at an initial range of 25,000 yards, but soon closing to 16,000. The British battleships blasted *Bismarck* with their ten 14-inch and nine 16-inch guns until 1015, when Tovey broke off the engagement to head

back north to refuel. By this time *Bismarck* was a battered hulk, ablaze from stem to stern, with all her guns silenced but her flag still flying proudly. Russell Grenfell has described the German battleship's end in vivid terms:

"By 10 am the *Bismarck* was a silent, battered wreck. Her mast was down, her funnel had disappeared, her guns were pointing in all directions, and a cloud of black smoke was rising from the middle of the ship and blowing away in the wind. Inside, she was clearly a blazing inferno, for the bright glow of internal fires could be seen shining through numerous shell and splinter holes in her sides. Her men were deserting their guns, and parties of them could be seen running to and fro on the upper deck as shells continued to rain in, and occasionally jumping over the side, to escape by a watery death from the terror on board. Captain Patterson would have ceased fire earlier had he known of this, but the *Bismarck's* port side was so screened by a wall of shell splashes along her whole length that it was none too easy to notice what was happening on board her."

Who actually sank *Bismarck*?

It should be pointed out here that there is a difference of opinion between British and German historians about the last few minutes of *Bismarck's* life. The British claim that the German battleship was finally sunk by two torpedoes from *Dorsetshire* at 1036. German historians do not dispute the time, but claim that *Bismarck* was scuttled by her crew, after all her armament had been knocked out, to prevent her falling into the hands of the British. What does seem clear, however, is that none of the British shells succeeded in penetrating *Bismarck's* belt or deck armour.

In any event, the conclusion of Sir John Tovey's report must command general agreement: "*Bismarck* fought an extremely courageous battle against greatly superior forces; in the best tradition of the old Imperial German Navy, she went down with her colours flying."

Dorsetshire and the destroyer *Maori* picked up 110 survivors, *U-74* three more who were clinging to a raft, and the German supply ship *Sachsenwald* two more. On hearing of the result of the

◁△ *On the bridge of the British cruiser* Suffolk *during the chase. It was* Suffolk *which sighted* Bismarck *and* Prinz Eugen *in the Denmark Strait, and* Suffolk *which lost radar contact with the German battleship while completing the outer leg of a zig-zag.*

◁▽ *The awesome power of a 15-inch salvo;* Bismarck *silhouettes herself from stem to stern with her own gun flashes.*

△ *1030 hours, May 26, and* Bismarck *is sighted by an R.A.F. Catalina in this Norman Wilkinson painting.*
▽ *Some of the survivors of* Bismarck *in the bitter oil-clogged waters of the North Atlantic. The* Dorsetshire *and the* Maori *picked up 110 men, but the rescue operations were restricted by the presence of German submarines.*

engagement, General Franco sent the Spanish cruiser *Canarias* to the area, but no further survivors were found.

The following points should be made in conclusion:

1. What would have been the result if the aircraft-carrier *Graf Zeppelin*, which had been launched in 1938, had been with *Bismarck*? Her Messerschmitt Bf 109T fighters would have made mincemeat of the British aircraft, and her Stukas could have played havoc with the British warships.

2. Without such an aircraft-carrier, the Luftwaffe was powerless to save *Bismarck*: the first Heinkel 111 to arrive on the scene did so a few minutes after *Bismarck* had gone down. The following day, however, German aircraft were able to sink the destroyer *Mashona*.

3. *Bismarck*'s and *Prinz Eugen*'s sortie had forced the British Admiralty to send in pursuit eight battleships and battle-cruisers, 11 cruisers, 22 destroyers, and six submarines, thus proving that Admiral Raeder's "Z-Plan" was basically sound. But what he did not possess in May 1941 was a combat force capable of utilising this forced redeployment of the Allied naval forces.

4. Throughout the 141 hours that the chase lasted, the fact that the Royal Navy lacked tankers able to refuel its warships at sea was, logistically and tactically, a constant headache both for Tovey and the Admiralty. It is in this light that Lieutenant-Commander Wolfahrt's exclamation "no destroyers, no zig-zags" takes on its full significance. Compare the British situation with Raeder's. At the same time, and in considerably more difficult circumstances, he had no fewer than 13 supply ships operating in the Atlantic, loaded with fuel, spare parts, and ammunition for *Bismarck*'s squadron, U-boats, and the disguised surface raiders.

Now alerted, the Admiralty sent out powerful forces, including the aircraft-carriers *Eagle* and *Victorious*, against them. Between June 5 and 18, nine of these supply ships were sunk, the four others managing to return to port but never to go to sea again.

Prinz Eugen, after leaving *Bismarck*, continued south and thence to Brest, where she arrived on June 1. Such was the baptism of fire of this cruiser, which was later to be blown up by the third atomic bomb on December 16, 1946.

CHAPTER 56
The Production Race

From the documents available today it is evident that the fortunes of war in the early months of 1942 were evenly matched between the two great alliances.

By July 1, 1942, in spite of their disappointments of the previous year, Hitler and Mussolini felt close to victory. It is true that they must have suspected that success had not crowned Admiral Yamamoto's recent venture at Midway on June 4, but Tokyo had hidden the extent of the Japanese defeat from the other two partners in the Axis, and the general situation thus appeared excellent: Sevastopol' was being mopped up, while the offensive which was aimed at taking the Wehrmacht on to Stalingrad, Baku, and Batumi had begun brilliantly, sweeping the feeble Russian defences before it; in the Mediterranean, Malta seemed to have been definitely reduced to impotence and the Duce, who had travelled to Derna bringing with him the conqueror's white horse, was impatiently expecting any hour the telegram from Field-Marshal Rommel which would enable him to make a triumphal entry into Cairo.

Three months later the German 6th Army had begun its exhausting street battle in the centre of Stalingrad, while in the Caucasus the 1st Army was advancing towards Groznyy only in fits and starts, and the first snow had appeared on the mountain crests.

At the same time, the aircraft based on Malta were beginning to exact a steadily more greedy toll of the supplies destined for the Axis forces which were still held up before El Alamein. These German and Italian troops, still nursing their wounds after their attempt to reach the Suez Canal, were aware that the enemy was growing stronger with every day that passed. Finally, in the Pacific, the Japanese, far from taking their revenge for Midway, had been reduced to the defensive

▽ *The raw stuff of modern war: inside a steel factory in the British isles. Without steel weapons could not be made, ships and tanks would be out of the question, and aircraft would be without engines and vital armour plating.*

△ *Exaggerated but in substance correct: a contemporary British poster compares Germany's armed forces with those of Britain and, in 1942, Britain and the United States.*

in the jungles of Guadalcanal.

To sum up, 1942 was not to see the fulfilment of spring's promises in any theatre in this gigantic conflict.

On August 27, as he came away from the funeral of the son of Admiral Horthy, Regent of Hungary, who had been killed in an aircraft accident, Count Ciano wrote in his diary that his German opposite number had lost some of his previous boastful confidence:

"Ribbentrop's tone is moderate, even though he continues to be optimistic. The German: 'The war is already won' of the old days has now become: 'We cannot lose this war'. He is obviously coming off his high horse. He gave no particulars, but he judges Russia to be a hard nut, very hard, and thinks that not even if Japan should attack her would she be entirely knocked out. He makes no forecasts on the length of the war; it might have a rapid conclusion, 'but one must not count too much on that'."

The fact is that, if Ribbentrop was thinking along these lines, he had lost sight of the plan upon which his Führer had decided in the summer of 1940, which was to complete the annihilation of the Soviet Union in 1941. And this was based on the assumption that he could rule out the intervention of the United States on the side of Britain until 1942. Yet Hitler and Mussolini had not kept to this timetable. Four days after Pearl Harbor, giving the *casus foederis* of the Tripartite Pact a generous interpretation, they had not waited for the Russian campaign to achieve a decisive result before declaring war against the United States, to President Roosevelt's great satisfaction.

The arsenal of democracy

Since the war on two fronts would continue without any reasonable possibility of forecasting its length, the industrial might of the United States would weigh more and more heavily in the balance of the opposed forces. During the "Arcadia" Conference, which took place between December 23, 1941 and January 14 of the following year, President Roosevelt and the British Prime Minister met at the White House. Churchill, backed up by Lord Beaverbrook, and with the determined support of Harry Hopkins, persuaded his ally to revise the war industries programme to which Roosevelt had agreed on the day following the Japanese attack. In every class of material, the figures would be substantially increased and the table (A) below reveals the size of the effort which the eloquence and the persuasive powers of his friend Winston Churchill had inclined the President to undertake.

In addition, it was decided to raise the production figure for American merchant shipping to eight million tons deadweight by 1942 and to aim at a figure of ten million for 1943. And thus it is not at all difficult to understand why Churchill, summarising these figures, wrote to Clement Attlee who was deputising for him in London these words at the end of his letter of January 4, 1942:

"Max [Lord Beaverbrook] has been magnificent and Hopkins a godsend. Hope you will be pleased with immense resultant increase in programme."

A

	FORECAST	1942	1943
WARPLANES	31 250	45 000	100 000
TANKS	29 550	45 000	75 000
ANTI-AIRCRAFT GUNS	8 900	20 000	35 000
ANTI-TANK GUNS	11 700	14 000	not fixed
MACHINE GUNS	238 000	500 000	not fixed

Göring refuses to believe it

Even though these figures had appeared in the message addressed by the President to Congress when he applied for the necessary supplementary credits, they aroused only incredulity and even derision among the leaders of the Third Reich. This was the origin of Ribbentrop's euphoria. Yet *Reichsmarschall* Göring himself, who as commander of the Luftwaffe and head of German industry ought to have been more alert, shared the general casualness about the war potential of the United States. This was noted with bitter irony by Erwin Rommel in the light of his recent experiences in North Africa. Leaving O.K.W. after a visit at the end of September 1942, he noted:

"During the conference I realised that the atmosphere in the Führer's H.Q. was extremely optimistic. Göring in particular was inclined to minimise our difficulties. When I said that the British fighter-bombers had shot up my tanks with 40-mm shells, the *Reichsmarschall*, who felt himself touched by this, said: 'That's completely impossible. The Americans only know how to make razor blades.' I replied: 'We could do with some of those razor blades, *Herr Reichsmarschall*.'

"Fortunately, we had brought with us a solid armour-piercing shell which had been fired at one of our tanks by a low-flying British aircraft. It had killed almost the entire crew."

But if Göring was so open in showing his scepticism about the American plan to build 45,000 warplanes in 1942, the reason was that he had on his desk the figures for the aeronautical industry of the Third Reich. In the same 12 months, with everything included, it delivered only 15,556 planes to the Luftwaffe. Göring based his opinion on this figure. In his mind, if Germany could, by stretching its energies to the limit, produce only 1,300 machines per month, the figures quoted in President Roosevelt's message to Congress could represent nothing more than a flight of pure imagination.

In this he was mistaken for, in 1944, Germany herself, under a terrifying hail of bombs and incendiary devices, would manufacture about 40,600 aircraft of all types, including more than 25,000 fighters.

Göring was even more misinformed for, in this war of alliances, account must be taken of the aircraft production of the

powers allied to Germany and to the United States. For all kinds of reasons, in 1942 British and Russian production was far greater than that of Italy and Japan. The table (B) below illustrates this disproportion.

As regards armoured equipment, the figures were even more out of proportion since Hitler, by his decision of January 23, 1942, had thought it sufficient to increase production to 600 vehicles a month (7,200 per year) while, in the same year, the U.S.S.R. put 20,000 into service,

△ *Part of the United States' huge contribution to the Allied war effort: a Lockheed Hudson is swayed aboard a cargo vessel to join others awaiting shipment to the hard-pressed Coastal Command in Britain.*

B		
AXIS	**ALLIES**	
GERMANY 15 556	**45 000** UNITED STATES	
ITALY 2 818	**17 385** GREAT BRITAIN	
JAPAN 2 700	**12 000** SOVIET UNION	
TOTAL **21 074**	**74 385** TOTAL	

△ *Work in progress in a British shipyard. While Great Britain could not hope to match the great production of the United States, she could manage to meet many of her own merchant and naval vessel needs, and pass on the technical and tactical lessons she had learnt in two and a half years of war to the United States.*

Great Britain constructed 8,611, and the United States 24,000. To sum up, at this period of the war, the powerful industry of the Reich was not yet mobilised to the same degree as that of its adversaries.

Since munitions were being manufactured at these rates, there is clearly great significance in the fact that, by the end of summer 1942, in spite of considerable and seemingly decisive successes that had taken them to the gates of India, to the streets of Stalingrad, and to within 40 miles of Alexandria, the Axis Powers and Japan had not carried out their plans in any theatre of operations or achieved their targets: Midway, the oilfields of the Caucasus, and the Suez Canal. If these had been won, the Axis would have swept the board. All this assumes, of course, that the United States could bring its enormous industrial potential to bear on the various battlefields, and in Europe and North Africa this also implied the elimination of the U-boat threat to North Atlantic communications. Yet this menace was never so great as in the first six months of 1942 and would not finally be overcome until the end of March 1943.

Italo-German relations strained

At this point in its development, World War II must be considered from another angle: since two alliances are concerned, the relations – good or bad – between the allies in both blocs should come under examination.

Hitler continued to have full confidence in his friend Benito Mussolini. In fact, the Italian dictator was probably the only man to receive the Führer's respect and even affection. However, Mussolini was no longer in a position to refuse anything to his ally in the Pact of Steel. Certainly, in private, he sometimes complained about the Germans and about the behaviour of their troops in Italy, and he would shout, as he did in the presence of his son-in-law on February 20: "Among the cemeteries, I shall some day build the most important of all, one in which to bury German promises."

He could, however, no longer refuse to

believe the prophecies communicated to him by the German dictator, either in person, as at Klessheim on April 29 and 30, or by letter, as after the fall of Tobruk, or through an intermediary such as Lieutenant-General von Rintelen, the German liaison officer attached to *Comando Supremo*.

In fact, Fascist Italy counted negatively in the balance sheet of the Third Reich and required, if she were to be kept in action, military investments that Germany found increasingly burdensome. The growing participation of the Wehrmacht in operations in the Mediterranean and North Africa provided increasing possibilities for friction and bitterness between the Italian and German generals. General, later Marshal, Ugo Cavallero, did indeed strive to maintain Italian strategy along German lines, but he met ferocious opposition from the very heart of the government. Count Ciano, for instance, described him in his diary as a "perfect buffoon", "servile lackey", "clown", "imbecile" and, the day after the defeat at El Alamein, as "really the one responsible for all our troubles". These accusations will be examined in more detail in their correct context, but it will be noted for the moment that the Duce's Minister of Foreign Affairs did not fail to

receive those generals who came to him to protest about decisions taken by the Chief-of-Staff of the *Comando Supremo*.

It is very difficult to divide the responsibilities fairly between Germans and Italians in the growing tension which became increasingly evident as the year wore on.

For a start it is clear that, like many French generals in 1940, a number of the Italian military leaders in 1941 thought that they would have to do no more than adapt their experiences of 1918 to the new conflict. Yet, from another point of view, though one may have the greatest admiration for the tactical vision, the decision, and the valour of Rommel, one must admit that he had none of the qualities needed in a good leader of allied forces, in the manner of Foch in 1918 or Eisenhower from 1942 onwards. One only has to read his letters and his war diaries to understand the hostile feelings he aroused in officers of the Italian Army. In contrast, Kesselring knew how to gain their trust. It has also been seen how Rommel did not play fair with them and was capable of going over the head of the *Comando Supremo* and appealing directly to *Oberkommando der Wehrmacht*.

If he had been at the peak of his physical powers, would Mussolini have been able

1942 witnessed the rapid growth of Allied air power, the types illustrated here receiving considerable production orders.

◁ The Boeing B-17 Flying Fortress, which was to be the backbone of the U.S. bomber forces in Europe, had been ordered in small numbers before the U.S. entered the war, but 1942 saw an enormous increase in orders. 12,700 machines were built up to 1945.

◁ ▽ R.A.F. ground crew load .5-inch ammunition into the magazine of a Bell P-39 Airacobra. The Airacobra, which featured an engine behind the pilot, was found unsuitable for operations in Western Europe, but some 5,000 of the 9,558 built were shipped to the delighted Russians.

▽ The redoubtable Hawker Typhoon, a failure as an interceptor, but superb as a ground attack machine. Experiments with rockets were carried out in 1942, and the weapons became standard in 1943.

▷ Republic P-47 Thunderbolts. These entered service in 1942, and more than 15,500 were built.

▷ △ The Bristol Beaufighter night fighter and strike aircraft entered service in 1940.

▽ *Mussolini peers through the sight of an Italian mortar. By 1942 his health was suffering considerably, and Italy was quickly reduced to the level of Germany's poor relation by her own inadequate military potential and Ciano's growing hostility towards the Third Reich.*

▷ △ *Though Germany had started the war with her industry not on a full war footing, as it was expected to last only a short time, by 1941 it was clear that Germany was in for a long war, and the first steps towards turning Germany's industry onto full scale war production were taken. The photograph shows an assembly line for heavy calibre guns in an ordnance factory.*
▷ ▽ *A German skilled engineering worker at his lathe. By this stage of the war, much of this kind of work was being performed by women in Great Britain.*

to control the situation? It is unlikely, considering his lack of method and his changes of mood. However, after a few alarms in the spring, he had to face a new challenge in September: that of his health, which was affected by a painful stomach ulcer and complicated by an amoebic infection. As a result, he was forced to allow his son-in-law to represent Fascist Italy at the Axis conferences that were held to discuss the implications of the Anglo-American landings in North Africa, and Count Ciano no longer believed in Hitler's star.

The last touch to the picture of Italo-German relations is added by the fissures that grew steadily deeper in the monolith of the Fascist Party itself, and were revealed by the crisis of July 25, 1943, when Mussolini was sacked. By then, outside the Party, the German alliance had as many opponents in Italy as there were Italians.

Japan's "parallel war"

It was more difficult to reach agreement on a war plan between the Axis and Japan than between the two English-speaking governments and the Soviet Union. For one thing, Berlin and Rome were given very little information on the strategic intentions of their Japanese ally. Not until March 15, 1942 does Ciano mention the subject in his diary. On that day he notes:

"In a conference with Indelli [Italian Ambassador in Tokyo] the Japanese have defined their plans. No attack on India, which would disperse their forces in a field that is too vast and unknown; no attack on Russia; an extension of the conflict towards Australia, where it is evident that the Americans and British are preparing a counter-attack."

Then the curtain fell again and, on May 9, the Italian Foreign Minister was reduced to looking at communiqués published in the press in order to obtain some idea of what had really happened in the Battle of the Coral Sea. Ciano records his perplexity, since the bulletins issued by the Japanese General Staff affected the honour of the Emperor himself:

"Therefore, they should not lie, although war lies are more or less like those that do not compromise the honour of a woman—permissible lies."

In fact, it seems that Tojo, in imitation of Mussolini, had never envisaged any other form of belligerency than "parallel war". He would fight with his allies but admitted no possibility of any strategic co-operation. His absolute ambition was limited to conquering what the Japanese called the perimeter of Greater Asia, which would place the "Greater East Asia Co-Prosperity Sphere" out of the range of any Anglo-American counter-attack and would allow it to expand in peace.

At one moment, it might have been believed that Hitler, Mussolini, and Tojo were fighting as a team. This was at the beginning of April 1942 when the Japanese fleet under Admiral Kondo steamed into the Indian Ocean and launched its aircraft to bomb Colombo and Trincomalee, in Ceylon. Were the Japanese preparing for an invasion of Ceylon, or of Madagascar, where the base of Diego-Suarez, if captured, would have allowed them to cut the vital supply line linking the British 8th Army to its base in the United Kingdom? This was the question being asked in London and Washington. But, as early as April 10, Kondo had set course for Japan and, on May 26, the very day that Rommel's Panzers thrust eastwards towards Tobruk, Vice-Admiral Nagumo's aircraft-carriers sailed in the same direction, their objective being Midway.

Nevertheless, on August 3, Marshal Cavallero met the Japanese military mission in Rome and took the opportunity to explain his views to General Shimazu. Of course, collaboration between the

Japanese Empire and the Axis could only have been indirect in most cases. Yet there was one place where it could have been of immediate value: the Indian Ocean. But, according to the notes which he took after the meeting, the Japanese general reserved his opinion. Besides, after the disaster at Midway, of which Cavallero had not been informed, it was too late.

Japan's selfishness

Relations between Japan and the Soviet Union were still conditioned by the clauses of the Non-Aggression Pact of April 13, 1941. By virtue of this agreement, Russian cargo vessels, crammed with war material furnished under the terms of Lend-Lease, sailed from ports on the Pacific Coast of the United States and, even after Pearl Harbor, continued to use the short cut to Vladivostok through the Japanese archipelago. This was not to say that Tojo had seriously given up his secret ambitions over the northern part of the island of Sakhalin and the maritime province of eastern Siberia. But, for his hopes

△ *With the increase in armament production went an increase in the men to use them. Here U.S. infantry clear an obstacle on an assault course. Note that they are wearing the new pattern helmet, standardised on June 9, 1941. The earlier 1917 pattern helmet, similar to the British one, continued to be worn until several months into 1942.*

to be realised, he would have to wait until the Wehrmacht had made his task easier by crushing and eliminating the Red Army.

As has been seen, the Japanese war effort was based on entirely egoistic considerations and, from the second half of 1942 onward, would allow the enemies of the Tripartite Pact Powers steadily increasing freedom in their choice of objectives. It would permit them to apply, with ever-greater effectiveness, the principle laid down between the British and the American Chiefs-of-Staff at their earliest consultations: "Germany First".

To sum up: in the totalitarian camp, the strategic maxim of the concentration of effort was not put into effect between the Axis Powers. This would have serious consequences.

Allied co-operation

In the Allied camp, the machinery of the alliance did not function without some moments of friction, but generally it ran much more smoothly and satisfactorily. Churchill put it thus:

"The enjoyment of a common language was of course a supreme advantage in all British and American discussions. The delays and often partial misunderstandings which occur when interpreters are used were avoided. There were however differences of expression, which in the early days led to an amusing incident.

The British Staff prepared a paper which they wish to raise as a matter of urgency, and informed their American colleagues that they wished to 'table it'. To the American Staff 'tabling' a paper meant putting it away in a drawer and forgetting it. A long and even acrimonious argument ensued before both parties realised that they were agreed on the merits and wanted the same thing."

Apart from their telephone conversations and their written correspondence, the British Premier and the President of the United States met no fewer than eight times between the end of December 1941 and February 1945, accompanied by their principal military, political, and administrative aides, to review the situation and make decisions about their common purpose. Since none of these conferences lasted for less than a week, it is reasonable to conclude that, every time they met, the two statesmen went over all outstanding questions. In this Anglo-American dialogue, it is evident that the last word belonged to Franklin D. Roosevelt but, for all that, Winston Churchill was not reduced to the pitiful rôle played by Mussolini in his talks with Hitler. In 1942 and 1943 Churchill's opinions on the second front convinced the American President and in addition, at a later date, the latter would show a rare spirit of military comradeship towards his ally.

As regards the conduct of operations, from the day following Pearl Harbor, the Chiefs-of-Staff committee began to function. In it, on the British side, were General

Sir Alan Brooke, appointed Chief of the Imperial General Staff on November 13, 1941, Admiral of the Fleet Sir Dudley Pound, and Air Chief-Marshal Sir Charles Portal. On the American side there were General George Catlett Marshall, Admiral Ernest J. King, recently promoted Head of Naval Operations in place of Admiral Stark, and General Henry H. Arnold of the United States Army Air Force. This committee formed what came to be known as the Combined Chiefs-of-Staff Committee.

Agreement was not always easy between these six high-ranking men, and discussion at times could be stormy. Was Admiral King an anglophobe, as was often declared in London? This would be overstating the case, but it seemed to him that British naval supremacy belonged to the past and he did not hesitate to tell Sir Dudley Pound so. Furthermore, the "Germany First" plan appealed to him much less than to General Marshall. Disagreements between the latter and Sir Alan Brooke, though not so bitter, were still very serious, for they were based on questions of principle. These two generals may have spoken the same tongue, but not the same language.

Differing strategic concepts

Like the majority of American generals, Marshall held to a classical system of war on the Napoleonic model, consisting of wiping out the main enemy forces, without bothering about what, in the language of debate, would be called "side issues". Brooke was far less definite; certainly he opposed Winston Churchill's preference for "small parcels", but the system of "direct strategy", in which his American colleague believed, did not seem to him to be the only road to victory; particularly so, since from that time until the moment when the Allies would be able to mount a large-scale attack, they ought not to allow the enemy to enjoy full and entire freedom of action. And hence, it seemed to Brooke, they should go in for minor and pinpricking operations which would begin on a small scale and grow steadily larger.

Winston Churchill's views were similar. In one of the notes which he composed on *Duke of York* for President Roosevelt he wrote, underlining the passage:

"What will harm us is for a vast United States Army of ten millions to be created which for at least two years while it was training would absorb all available supplies and stand idle defending the American continent."

In this controversy, Marshall referred to the precedent of the first war of continental dimensions in which the U.S.A. had been involved, its own Civil War of 1861–1865, while Brooke, naturally enough, quoted the method by which Great Britain had defeated Napoleon in one great battle, the last. Nevertheless, it still remained to be seen whether the Russian campaign would have the same effect on the Wehrmacht as it had had on the armies of the French Emperor 120 years earlier.

In spite of these differences, co-operation between the British and American staffs was maintained permanently by the British Military Mission stationed in the

▽ *The American transport* General H. W. Butner *about to be launched. The U.S., fighting on the far side of the Pacific and Atlantic Oceans from their centres of production and manpower, were compelled to build large numbers of transports such as* Butner *to move and supply their scattered forces.*

УРАЛ

ФРОНТУ

△ *Soviet Russia, more perhaps than any other combatant nation, performed miracles of production. But Russia had not the technical skills to produce any but the more basic weapons, and relied on Britain and the United States for more sophisticated weapons and equipment. The poster above glorifies the war production that will halt the Germans.*

absolute loyalty. Yet it should not be assumed that Great Britain was the only partner to benefit from their co-operation. Actually, the United States owed her ally a great debt in tactical and technical expertise. The fact that the Prime Minister put the whole of the progress achieved by Great Britain in the field of nuclear arms into the President's hands, alone demonstrates the importance of the British contribution to the alliance.

Co-operation with Russia

With the Axis astride Europe from the North Cape to the Gulf of Sirte, relations between the Western Allies and the Russians were not easy. Churchill made his first contact with Stalin in August 1942, travelling from Cairo to Moscow. Then came the inter-Allied meetings at Teheran in November 1943, Yalta in February 1945, and Potsdam in July 1945, during which the three men responsible for the policies and strategy of the great Allied powers took the opportunity to put their points of view on the war and how it should be fought. This history will include discussion of the controversies which arose between Churchill, Roosevelt, and Stalin concerning the second front and the Arctic convoys.

However, generally speaking, military co-operation between the British, the Americans, and the Russians produced satisfactory results from the outset. Leaving aside the *matériel* of all kinds supplied to the U.S.S.R. under the Lend-Lease agreement, which will be described later, a simple comparison of two figures makes it clear that, on the eve of the invasion of Normandy, the strategy devised by the Combined Chiefs-of-Staff had already caused serious harm to the forces of the Wehrmacht fighting the Red Army.

On June 22, 1941, of his 208 divisions, Hitler had left 55 in occupied Europe and Libya, between the North Cape and Halfaya Pass. On June 5, 1944, though German land forces had in fact increased to 304 divisions, the defence of Norway, Denmark, the Netherlands, Belgium, France, Italy, the Balkans, Crete, and Rhodes absorbed 108 of them. This was not all, for, though the beginning of "Barbarossa" brought 34 out of 36 armoured and motorised divisions into action against Russia, on the day of Operation "Overlord", O.K.H. could deploy only 30 such units

American capital and headed by Sir John Dill from the end of December 1941. In that way a satisfactory and even neat solution was found for the chronically irritating conflict which had arisen between the ex-Chief of the Imperial General Staff and Churchill since the former's appointment some time earlier. His successor would have a task which was relatively easier because Winston Churchill no longer had the right to make decisions on his own on an impulse or momentary flash of inspiration.

In spite of these inevitable differences of view, the Chiefs-of-Staff Committee did excellent work and co-operated with between the Black Sea and the Baltic, while O.K.W. controlled 12 in France and six in Italy. It does not seem unreasonable to state that these figures speak for themselves.

As has been seen, on the technical side there were no secrets between the British and the Americans. They kept hardly any from their Soviet ally. This is revealed by General John R. Deane, who directed the American Military Mission in Moscow, under Ambassador W. Averell Harriman, from November 1943:

"Our policy was to make any of our new inventions in electronics and other fields available to the Russians once we had used such equipment ourselves, had exploited the element of surprise, and were satisfied that the enemy had probably gained knowledge of the equipment as a result of its having fallen into his hands. Each month I would receive a revised list of secret American equipment about which the Russians could be informed in the hope that, if it could be made available, it might be used on the Russian front. We never lost an opportunity to give the Russians equipment, weapons, or information which we thought might help our combined war effort."

But General Deane confesses that this collaboration was one-way only. The Russians grew steadily less inclined to give information even on the nature and quality of material captured from the Germans.

The British, for their part, were stupefied when faced with Moscow's blank refusal to allow them to set up a hospital at Archangel where British medical staff would have tended sailors wounded aboard cargo ships bringing arms and munitions, through extreme danger, to Britain's Soviet ally.

Hitler repudiates the rules of war

From 1942 the conflict between the two mighty alliances became more bitter.

On June 9, 1941, two weeks before he unleashed Operation "Barbarossa", Hitler informed his generals that, in the struggle he was leading against Bolshevism, he could not consider himself bound by those rules of international law which attempt to ease the harsher aspects of war. Certainly, he said, the enemy would not respect them. Consequently he refused to grant prisoner-of-war status to commissars of the Red Army who fell into German hands, and ordered that they were to be shot on the spot.

It is true that this order came up against the opposition of the majority of German generals, who, like Manstein, considered that it was "contrary to the military spirit" and, if carried out, "would not only stain the honour of the troops but affect

△ A pre-war photograph of General Draža Mihailović, leader of the Royalist guerrillas in Yugoslavia, the Četniks. Soon, however, they were to be involved in a war with Tito's communist partisans as much as with the German forces occupying their country.

▽ In Russia too, partisan units sprang up behind the German lines, and were fostered assiduously by the Russian High Command. In time these partisan forces were to prove a very serious problem for the Germans, who were forced to waste large numbers of men policing their lines of communication.

their morale". So they concealed the order and permitted their subordinates to do likewise. But this instruction, which shocked officers brought up in the old military tradition, received the enthusiastic approval of the Nazis in charge of administering the conquered territories and of the S.S. units responsible for enforcing the "New Order".

On its side equally, the guerrilla warfare which had flared up behind the German lines did not respect the customs of war as prescribed by international law. Nor could it be expected to do so, for it would be difficult to expect the partisans, not wearing uniform, fighting a war of ambushes and sabotage hundreds of miles behind the lines, to organise prisoner-of-war camps regularly inspected by delegates of the International Red Cross! And so there followed a hideous war which, on both sides, usually involved the killing of the wounded and of prisoners.

In Yugoslavia, war was now widespread, mainly in Serbia and Montenegro. On one side, supported by King Peter II and the Yugoslav Government in exile, General Draža Mihailović, who had never surrendered, continued to wage guerrilla war against the invaders of his country. On the other, the German attack of June 22, 1941 had authorised Comrade Josip Broz, alias "Tito", an ex-recruiting sergeant for the Popular Front in Paris and member of the *Comintern*, to emerge from the calm tranquillity with which he had contemplated the national catastrophe of the previous spring.

But General Mihailović's *Četniks* and the partisans of the future Marshal Tito were themselves sworn enemies, for the latter were aiming not merely at the defeat of the German invaders but also at installing a Communist régime in Belgrade. So, from the end of 1941, Yugoslavia suffered a pitiless civil war grafted on to its war against Germany. On Hitler's orders, the Germans did not differentiate between *Četniks* and communist partisans, and waged a war of extermination against both. Meanwhile, General Roatta, commander of the Italian 2nd Army, attempted to establish some sort of understanding with the *Četniks*, who were not deaf to his blandishments. This difference in their treatment of the Yugoslavs gave rise to acrimonious correspondence between the two Axis partners.

Women at War

As the war progressed, women were used in ever increasing numbers as part of British industrial "manpower", thus releasing men for service in the armed services. The contribution to the Allies' final victory by such women in Britain, the Empire and Commonwealth, the United States, and Russia was thus very real and important. Besides industrial work, women also worked on the land and kept such vital services as the post and telephones working.

◁◁ A woman lathe-operator in a British munitions factory—compare this with the German man doing a similar job in the photograph on page 765.

◁ A woman at work in an aircraft factory connecting up the hydraulic lines in an undercarriage system.

▷ A scene typical of thousands: dinghies for aircraft crew being manufactured by women war workers.

The resistance movements emerge

In the Scandinavian and western European countries occupied by the Germans, the main activity of the resistance movements up to then had been the gathering of information and aiding British or Polish personnel stranded by the tide of war. Great importance must be attached to the information about the Germans discovered by the Norwegian, Danish, Dutch, Belgian, and French networks. Briefly, from 1941 onwards, Hitler could not move a division or a warship, or begin fortification work, without London learning of it in the minimum of time.

Communism takes a hand

On June 22 of the same year, the Communist parties of the occupied countries went over to resistance, following the German attack just launched on the Soviet Union. Their contribution was without doubt of vital importance. The unquestioning discipline of their adherents, their unshakable determination to serve Moscow, the fact that they were accustomed to working clandestinely, and their long practice in espionage made them redoubtable fighters in this secret war; on the other hand, there is reason to doubt the efficiency of all the actions against the invader undertaken by such forces.

The murder of some German soldiers or officers in a passage in the Paris Metro or in a dark street in Nantes had not the slightest effect on the capacities of the Wehrmacht, but for the French people it signified frightful reprisals. Furthermore the enforcement of security measures that such murders brought in their wake itself hindered the action of the resistance fighters. Similarly, there are legitimate doubts about the advantages of assassinating Reinhard Heydrich, Chief of the Reich Security Head Office, which comprised the *Gestapo*, S.P., and S.D. Heydrich was the abominable successor to Baron von Neurath at the head of the "Protectorate" of Bohemia and Moravia. Yet the death of this undoubted criminal,

△ *Reinhard Heydrich, chief of the Reich Security Head Office, comprising the* Geheime Staatspolizei *or Gestapo (Secret State Police), the* Sicherheitspolizei *(Security Police), and the* Sicherheitsdienst *(Security Service of the S.S.). Eager for more power, he had himself appointed Acting Protector of Bohemia and Moravia, the Protector, Neurath, being sent on indefinite leave as he was "sick". On May 29, 1942 Heydrich's car was ambushed by two Czechs parachuted in from England. A bomb was hurled at the car and Heydrich received fatal wounds. He died on June 4, and the reprisals started immediately.*

once dismissed from the *Kriegsmarine* for misconduct, was paid for by savage reprisals, including the extermination of the entire male population of the Czech village of Lidice.

Hitler denies the Geneva Convention

Up to this moment, the war between the armies of Germany, France, Britain, Belgium, Holland, and Norway, though brutal, had not gone past the limits set by the Geneva Convention. But in 1942 British raids against Saint Nazaire (on March 28), Dieppe (on August 19), and Tobruk (on the night of September 13-14) so exasperated Hitler that, on October 18, he issued his famous order regarding commandos. Claiming that these units were recruited in United Kingdom prisons and that they had received orders to execute their prisoners, the Führer ordered the same treatment to be applied to them:

"From now on, all enemy personnel taking part in operations described as 'commando', against German forces in Europe and North Africa, are to be executed to the last man, whether they are soldiers wearing uniform of sorts, or demolition groups armed or unarmed, fighting or in flight."

Of course, nobody would deny that British troops were not gentle in their fighting techniques; but, between neatly stabbing or strangling a sleepy sentry and coldly ordering the shooting of a helpless prisoner, there is all the difference between an act of war which is cruel but legitimate and perhaps necessary, and a war crime specifically proscribed by the Geneva Convention.

On December 13, 1942, this criminal order was applied to Lieutenant Mackinnon of the Royal Marines and four of his companions who had paddled up the Gironde river in two-seater kayaks and blown up with limpet mines five German cargo ships moored in Bordeaux harbour. But all the evidence goes to show that such cases were exceptional or almost so, as German troops found these evil procedures repugnant.

Nevertheless the order of October 18, 1942 was still held against Field-Marshal Keitel and Colonel-General Jodl by the International War Crimes Tribunal at Nuremberg. These two men had countersigned Hitler's order and transmitted it for action by their subordinates. It contributed in no small way to the death sentence which was pronounced on them.

Russia hits back

offensive, Hitler, who had taken over control of O.K.H. and the Eastern Front from Field-Marshal von Brauchitsch, issued the following order to his armies on December 28.

"The abandonment without struggle of positions, even if they have been only cursorily prepared, leads, under present weather conditions, to intolerable losses in material and munitions. It weakens our fighting capacities and allows the enemy ever-growing freedom of action."

In order to exploit to the full the defensive situation to which he was for the moment reduced, he ordered every village and even every farmhouse to be made into a stronghold, with garrisons drawn from all fighting arms and also from the service échelons. Over a wide expanse of territory, this "quartering" of the terrain—to use General Weygand's expression of the end of May 1940—would force the enemy to bivouac in the open, prevent him using his road and rail network, and finally reduce him to impotence and famine.

Nevertheless, to redeploy in depth, as the order required, the heavily-stretched German units, who were already fighting on an excessively long front, were obliged to spread their resources even more thinly. And so the enemy was able to filter through the gaps which inevitably opened in their lines. In fact the Russians were able to penetrate the German front even more easily than they would have been able to do in summer, because the extreme temperatures had frozen the lakes and rivers to the extent that they no longer formed

△ *Huddled in their greatcoats, these German infantrymen stumble forward over Russia's frozen steppe. Under such terrible conditions, Russian reinforcements, many of them Siberians used to the cold, were doubly effective.*
▷ *The negation of modern war: where motors would not run, both sides had recourse to the old Russian methods of transport— trains of sledges pulled by horses.*

On January 1, 1942, between Feodosiya, on the south side of the Crimea, and Oranienbaum on the Gulf of Finland, 12 German armies (with 141 divisions, six of them from satellite countries, plus five Hungarian and Rumanian brigades) were locked in combat with 22 Soviet armies (a total of 328 divisions or their equivalent).

Even temperatures of 30 and even 40 degrees below zero, recorded from one end to the other of the front, and 1,000 miles difference in latitude, did not force the Russians to seek winter quarters. On the contrary, during the month of January, Stalin would extend his offensive to the left and right flanks of the front, no longer limiting himself to Army Group "Centre", against which Generals Konev and Zhukov continued to struggle, with 165 divisions confronting Kluge's 68.

In the face of this first Soviet winter

obstacles. Their ice was so thick that it could even support 52-ton heavy tanks.

To stiffen the German line, which was buckling and threatening to break at any moment, Hitler called on troops from Occupied France and others who had just finished their training in Germany. Between the end of December 1941 and the end of March 1942, no less than 22 infantry divisions were moved from West to East for this purpose.

Moreover, the situation was so dangerous in certain sectors that they were thrown into action as soon as they detrained, in small groups and without time to distribute equipment and clothing to withstand the climate. For its part, the Red Army was reinforced in the first six months of 1942 by the addition of about 60 new divisions.

The offensive against Army Group "Centre"

In a directive dated January 7, 1942, the Soviet High Command ordered Generals Konev and Zhukov, in command of the Kalinin and West Fronts respectively, to go over once more to the attack, with the intention of annihilating Army Group "Centre".

For this purpose the forces of the Kalinin Front would move forward along the Ostashkov–Volga line, attacking in a general south-westerly direction and, to

the west of Vyaz'ma, would cut the road and railway between Minsk and Moscow, the life-lines of Army Group "Centre". Furthermore, using the gap which had been formed during the retreat to the south of Kaluga between the right wing of the German 4th Army and the left wing of 2nd *Panzerarmee*, the West Front would make its main effort in the direction of Vyaz'ma. This gigantic pincer-movement, aimed at bringing about the encirclement of the whole of Army Group "Centre", would be covered on its right by attacks by troops of the North-West Front and on its left by offensives by the Bryansk Front.

The offensive so planned made an excellent beginning on January 9 and 10, 1942. For three weeks, O.K.H. was seriously concerned that Konev and Zhukov should meet in the region of Dorogobuzh, some 16 miles south of the Moscow–Minsk railway.

Eremenko pushes through

In the north, the 4th Shock Army (General A. I. Eremenko), which formed the right of the Kalinin Front, took advantage of the thick ice on Lake Seliger, the boundary between Army Groups "Centre" and "North", to break through the German lines which, in this sector, were no more than skeletal. Eremenko pushed straight as far as Velikiye-Luki, more than 115 miles from his starting-point, replenishing his supplies from depôts which the

△ A Russian poster of 1942: "Defend Mother Volga". But the Soviet winter and spring offensives meant that this vital river barrier, which Hitler had intended his armies to reach in their first thrust into Russia, would now be safe until the end of August 1942—and then the river's major town, Stalingrad, was to prove the graveyard of Germany's Russian adventure.

775

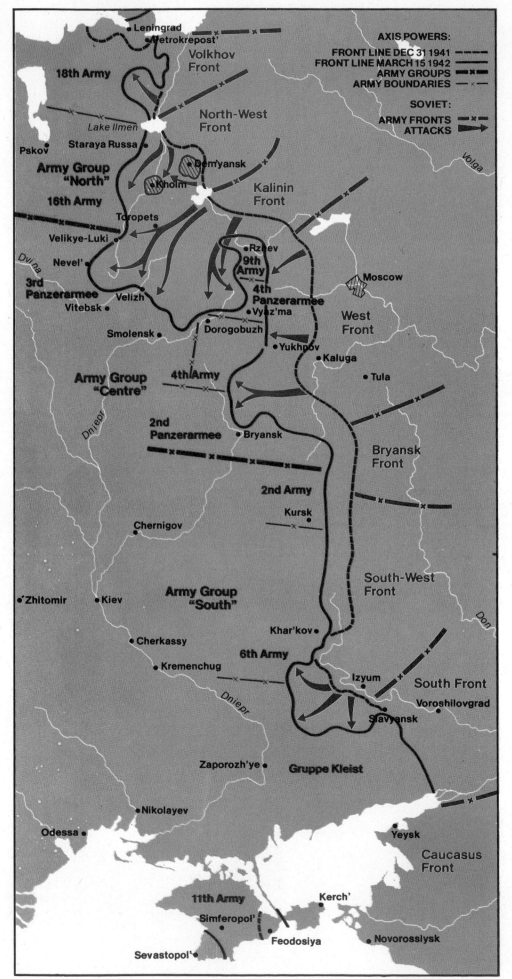

AXIS POWERS:
FRONT LINE DEC 31 1941 – – – –
FRONT LINE MARCH 15 1942 ————
ARMY GROUPS ✕✕✕✕
ARMY BOUNDARIES —✕—✕

SOVIET:
ARMY FRONTS ✕✕✕✕
ATTACKS ➤

Germans had built up at Toropets. In this way the Russians made up for the defects of the Soviet supply services, which had failed to keep up with the front line units. On February 1, however, 3rd *Panzerarmee* (Colonel-General Reinhardt) retook the line Demidov–Velizh–Nevel'–Velikiye-Luki and blocked the Russians' potentially dangerous advance to Vitebsk and Smolensk.

29th Army cut off

In the centre of the Kalinin Front, General Konev separated his 29th, 39th, and 30th Armies which, to the west of Rzhev, had succeeded in splitting the German 9th Army and isolating its left wing, which consisted of the XXIII Corps (General Schubert). The Soviet 29th Army exploited its breakthrough to the full, and, on January 27, was within tactical reach of the Minsk–Moscow road. But General Walther Model, who had just taken over command of 9th Army, was an astonishing military improviser. Ignoring the various concentrated offensives against Rzhev from the north and east, he counter-attacked vigorously in a westerly direction and established contact with XXIII Corps at the end of the month. Now it was the turn of the Soviet 29th Army to find its communications cut. In the course of the subsequent furious battles, it lost 27,000 dead and 5,000 prisoners. Only 5,000 men, 800 of whom were wounded, managed to break out of the pocket and reach Soviet lines on February 15.

"German casualties, too, had been heavy," Paul Carell notes. "On February 18, when *Obersturmbannführer* Otto Kumm reported at his divisional headquarters, Model happened to be there. He said to Kumm: 'I know what your regiment has been through–but I still can't do without it. What is its present strength?'

"Kumm gestured towards the window. *'Herr Generaloberst*, my regiment is on parade outside.' Model glanced through the window. Outside, 35 men had fallen in.'"

Model's gift for manoeuvre and his prompt decision had therefore carried the day against Russian doggedness, for the Russian 39th Army was as sore-hit as the Germans. Nevertheless, Model's army was trapped in a tube-shaped pocket nearly 125 miles long and, in the region of Sychevka, barely 40 miles in width.

It was now vital that Rzhev be evacuated, if only to allow the 12 or so divisions earmarked for the summer offensive the chance to recuperate. Yet before he would consent, Hitler delayed until the reverse at Stalingrad put the seal on his defeat.

Hitler consents to a retreat

On the other hand, on January 15, in view of the speedy and dangerous advances by the 49th, 50th, and 10th Armies of the West Front into the breach which had been opened south of Kaluga, Hitler authorised Kluge to order the necessary withdrawals to permit the left of 2nd *Panzerarmee* to link-up firmly again with the right of 4th Army:

"This is the first time in the war," his order concluded, "that I have ordered a withdrawal over a sizable section of the front. I expect the movement to be carried out in a manner worthy of the German Army. Our men's confidence in their innate superiority and their absolute determination to cause the enemy as much damage as possible must also condition the way in which this withdrawal is carried out."

In order to slow down enemy pursuit, the Germans, just as the Russians had done previously, applied a scorched earth policy to the areas they abandoned. Villages were razed, and even the stoves used to heat the Russian dwellings were destroyed at Hitler's express order.

Zhukov's advance blocked

General Zhukov's offensive followed a pattern similar to Konev's. A lightning jump-off took I Guard Cavalry Corps almost to Dorogobuzh, but there the advance was checked, causing a stabilised front to develop. At the end of February, Field-Marshal von Kluge had redeployed

▽ *The pattern of Russian attacks: intense artillery bombardment and close co-operation by aircraft such as the Shturmoviks seen flying over this gun.*
▽ ▽ *Winter war in Russia – temperatures dropping to 40 degrees below zero Centigrade and logistics based on horse and sledge.*

◁ ◁ A Pzkw III of the 11th Panzer Division leads its comrades forward into action. Note the Panzergrenadiers advancing, sheltered by their armour.

◁ Part of a German infantry section makes use of the natural cover given by a small dip in the ground to give supporting fire for an infantry attack.

◁ ▽ A sorry sight for the crew of this German armoured car: Narvik, 1,700 kilometres away, Athens, 2,220 kilometres away, and Brest, 2,910 kilometres away were all in German hands. Moscow, which was only 100 kilometres distant, was never to fall to the German Army.

▽ Scorched earth in reverse. As they were forced back, the Germans adopted the earlier Russian policy of destroying all that they could not take with them.

after his withdrawal and re-established a continuous front along the Kirov–Yukhnov line. As a result, General Pliev's I Guard Cavalry Corps was trapped and, slightly more to the north, a similar fate overtook the 33rd Army. Russian G.H.Q. in Moscow tried to get the operation moving again by parachuting two brigades behind the German lines and extending General Zhukov's authority to include the Kalinin Front. But Army Group

under the assault of the 3rd Shock Army (General Purkaev) emerging from the Lake Seliger region, and the 11th Army (General Morosov), which swept over the frozen Lake Ilmen.

Certainly the latter, in spite of five furious attacks, was halted before Staraya Russa, but working its way up the Lovat' it succeeded, on February 8, in closing the trap around the German II Corps. This formed a 200 mile pocket around Dem'yansk, which was defended by five badly-worn divisions. But, under the command of General Brockdorff-Ahlefeldt, they repelled every enemy attack, even when the Russians parachuted two brigades into the centre of the pocket. To supply the 96,000 men and their 20,000 horses, the Luftwaffe organised an airlift. At a rate of 100 to 150 aircraft daily, it brought the besieged men more than 65,000 tons of foodstuffs, forage, munitions, and fuel, also flying out over 34,500 wounded and sick.

The Kholm pocket

On March 21, General Seydlitz-Kurzbach moved out of Staraya Russa and attacked with four divisions in the direction of Dem'yansk. An unexpected thaw hampered this movement and not till April 21 was he able to re-establish contact with II Corps across the Lovat'. Some 65 miles south-west of Dem'yansk, the little town of Kholm and its garrison, commanded by Major-General Scherer, was cut off by the 3rd Shock Army. The pocket was relieved just as it was about to fall.

The actions at Kholm and Dem'yansk must be put very much on the debit side of the Red Army's account book. And furthermore, the operation laid down for the Volkhov Front (General Meretskov) ended in disaster for the 2nd Shock Army.

Failure before Leningrad

Under the command of General Vlasov, 2nd Shock Army, six divisions strong, crossed the Volkhov on January 22 and pushed north-east, reaching the Leningrad–Novgorod railway. The attack was to take place at the same time as an offensive by the 54th Army, emerging from the area south-east of Petrokrepost'. If the manoeuvre had succeeded, the salient

△ △ *General von Seydlitz-Kurzbach, whose drive from Staraya Russa lifted the siege of the Dem'yansk pocket. The successful defence and air supply of the pocket was hailed as a considerable success at the time – and so it was, tactically. But it led the Germans to believe that it could be repeated on a larger, strategic level, and thus sowed the seeds of the terrible defeat at Stalingrad.*
△ *A German MG 34 machine gun crew. Behind them is evidence that the Russians did not have things all their own way – a knocked-out T-26 tank.*

"Centre" still maintained its positions along the Minsk–Vyaz'ma and Vyaz'ma–Rzhev lines.

The *History of the Great Patriotic War* does not conceal the slowing down of this winter offensive, from which Stalin had expected a decisive victory. It blames its failure on to the fact that the armies of the West Front wasted their shock value by attacking over fronts which were too long. This is very likely, but the question must be considered at a higher level than the one set by the *Great Patriotic War*. It would appear that the principles of concentration of force and convergence of effort were both insufficiently understood in the highest councils of *Stavka*, as Russian G.H.Q. was called.

Beginning on January 8, to the north of the Kalinin Front, General Kurochkin, commander of the North-West Front, badly mauled the German 16th Army, which formed the right wing of Army Group "Centre". The 16th Army broke

△ *German 10.5-cm light field howitzers being readied for action. Note the members of the crew stacking up ammunition just behind the trail.*

◁ *"Let us bend all our technical capabilities against the arrogant enemy." Russian industry was now getting back to full production, but the Red Navy, for all the vigour expressed in this poster, played only a small part in the war.*

ОБРУШИМ ВСЮ СИЛУ МОГУЧЕЙ БОЕВОЙ ТЕХНИКИ ПРОТИВ НАГЛОГО ВРАГА.

formed here by the German 18th Army would have been liquidated and Leningrad relieved at the same time. But the 54th Army failed in the face of the resistance of I Corps (March 10, 1942).

From that moment on, Vlasov, who had been reinforced by the XIII Cavalry Corps and three armoured brigades and had deployed his forces fanwise, found himself in a very risky situation, for the handle of the fan was only 13 miles wide while his forward troops were 50 miles from the Volkhov. From March 15 to March 19, furious combat, in which the Spanish volunteers of the *División Azul* distinguished themselves, allowed the German 18th Army to sever the line which joined the 2nd Shock Army to the main Soviet line. The mopping-up operations lasted until the end of May. Vlasov himself was not captured until the end of July.

Success in the south

In the southern theatre of operations, the sudden death of Field-Marshal von Reichenau led Hitler to entrust the command of Army Group "South" to Field-Marshal von Bock. As he entered his office at Poltava on January 18, the new commander of German operations in the Ukraine and the Crimea was received with two pieces of news. One was good: Feodosiya had been recaptured by General von Manstein, who had also taken 10,000 prisoners. This would allow the siege of Sevastopol' to continue without fear of being surprised by Russian attack. The other news was disturbing: the 17th Army's front had been pierced near Izyum.

General von Manstein recalls the difficulties which arose at the time of the recapture of Feodosiya and also his attitude about the treatment of Russian P.O.W.s:

"Everything seemed to have conspired against us. Extremely severe frosts affected the airfields at Simferopol' and Yevpatoriya, which were used by our Stukas and bombers, and often prevented aircraft taking off in the morning to attack Feodosiya. The Kerch' Strait was frozen over and allowed free passage to enemy units.

"In spite of the difficulties, the army did its best to feed—sometimes even reducing its own rations—the prisoners whom we had not sufficient transport to transfer north. Consequently, the mortality rate among the prisoners averaged only two per cent. This was an extremely low figure, considering that most of them were seriously wounded or absolutely exhausted at the time of their capture. One incident may serve to illustrate their feelings towards us. There was a camp for 8,000 prisoners close to Feodosiya when the Russians made their landing. The camp guards fled, but the prisoners, instead of running towards their 'liberators', set off, without guards, towards Simferopol', towards us, that is."

On the Donets, Marshal Timoshenko, in command of the South-West Front, had attacked seven German divisions with his 37th, 57th, and 6th Armies, totalling 21 infantry divisions, 11 cavalry divisions, and ten armoured brigades (about 650 tanks). The long-range object of this operation was Khar'kov and the railway between Dniepropetrovsk and Donetsk (Stalino), which supplied the German 17th Army and 1st *Panzerarmee*. In temperatures of 40 degrees below zero the Russians spread out behind the German line and, by January 26, were restocking their supplies from the stores which the 17th Army had established at Lozovaya. Two days later they reached Sinel'nikovo and Grishino, which were within gunshot of the railway they hoped to cut. Several days later they were thrown back by *Gruppe* von Kleist which was an amalgamation of Kleist's own 1st *Panzerarmee* and the 17th Army.

The Russian attack then folded up. Army Group "South" had indeed had a nasty shock, but Timoshenko had not been able to widen the breach he had made on the Donets front on January 18. The Izyum salient, about 60 miles deep, would cause him the same tragic disaster as the Volkhov salient had brought on Vlasov.

◁ ◁ *Russian dead. But whereas the Germans were to find the problem of getting replacements increasingly difficult, Russia, with her considerably greater population and more stoical attitude to casualties, was able to keep her divisions supplied with men.*
◁ ▽ *German dead around an 8-cm mortar. During this appalling cold winter, the effective strength of some German regiments fell as low as 35 men.*
▽ *Even the spring did not at first bring respite to the Germans. The thaw brought back mud similar to that which had crippled the first offensive in the autumn of the previous year.*

△ *A column of German infantry on the move. The improved weather of late spring gave the Germans the opportunity to use their superior tactical skills to halt the Russian offensive.*

▽ *The ever-present threat to German communications – "Partisans, fight the enemy without pity!"*

The weather forces a truce

From March 21, mud steadily replaced snow between the shores of the Baltic and the Black Sea, making any significant operations impossible for close on two months. This relative truce allowed the two adversaries to consider their achievements and lay their plans for the coming summer campaign.

According to statistics calculated by O.K.H., over the entire Eastern Front the Germans had lost, between January 1 and March 20, a little more than 240,000 men, of whom 51,837 had been killed and 15,086 were missing. This brought their losses since June 22, 1941 to 1,073,006 officers, N.C.O.s, and men, that is just under one-third of the effectives who had attacked on that date. It is true that the Wehrmacht had escaped the disaster which had just threatened it, but only just, and, to a large extent, because of the fact that *Stavka* had not been able to concentrate its efforts to exclusively to destroying Army Group "Centre".

And so Colonel-General Halder, not exhibiting at this time any sign of pessimism in general, recommended prudence to the new Commander-in-Chief of the German Army. But it was not for lack of caution that Hitler had dismissed Brauchitsch. Since the Soviet winter offensive had been more or less checked, all risks appeared laudable to the Führer and, for six months, he could be heard shouting as he stared at the campaign maps: "*Der Russe ist tot! Der Russe ist tot!* (Russia is dead! Russia is dead!)".

Even today information on Soviet losses in this period is unavailable. However, everything seems to indicate that these were considerable, even more so as the rear-guard services of the Red Army functioned very badly and the Russians were not so insensitive to the cold as their opponents thought. As Lieutenant Goucharov noted:

"January 25. 'You know, Comrade Lieutenant,' one of my men said to me yesterday, 'when one gets really cold one becomes indifferent to freezing to death or being shot. One only has one wish – to die as quickly as possible.' That's the exact truth. The cold drains the men of the will to fight."

CHAPTER 58
Java Sea & Singapore

On September 11, 1941, General Marshall and Admiral Stark sketched out to President Roosevelt the "main lines of the military policy" which they thought should be adopted, and proposed that these should be implemented without delay. In this extensive document they drew the President's attention to the enormous danger that the Third Reich would be to America if it were given the time to re-organise the continent of Europe as it liked. They therefore both agreed:

"The principal strategic method employed by the United States in the immediate future should be the material support of present military operations against Germany, and their reinforcement by active participation in the war by the United States while holding Japan in check pending future developments."

For this purpose, the "maintenance of an active front in Russia" appeared extremely important to them, and it was also imperative to "prevent Axis penetration into North Africa and the islands of the Atlantic" (Cape Verdes, Canaries, Madeira, and Azores).

These proposals, which were accepted by the President, also met the wishes of the British cabinet. In effect, Hitler and Mussolini, by declaring war on the United States, had saved Roosevelt the difficulty of persuading Congress that the best way to avenge Pearl Harbor would be to have two more new enemies on America's hands. Nevertheless, just when Churchill was preparing to put the case for Operation "Gymnast" (an American landing in Algeria in conjunction with an 8th Army drive into Tunisia) to the men responsible for American strategy, it was already apparent to the latter that their forces were unable to keep Japan at bay anywhere in the Far East.

But this order of priorities, in which the defeat of Germany would take priority over that of Japan, was not questioned by Roosevelt, Marshall, and Stark at the "Arcadia" Conference in Washington at the end of 1941. On the contrary, Marshall and Stark (the latter of whom was later replaced by Admiral Ernest J. King) took up an unequivocal position on the matter from the time of their first meeting with their British colleagues:

". . . notwithstanding the entry of Japan into the war, our view remains that Germany is still the prime enemy and her defeat is the key to victory. Once Germany is defeated the collapse of Italy and the defeat of Japan must follow."

Agreement was reached on the principle of such a landing on January 12, whereupon the plan was reworked as "Super-Gymnast". According to this new version, three British and three American divisions were to land in Morocco and Algeria from April 15 onwards. At the same time, three more American divisions would cross the Atlantic and relieve three British divisions in Northern Ireland. The latter

△ Fleet Admiral Ernest J. King, who replaced Stark as C.-in-C., Navy. Despite his concern for the Pacific war, he endorsed the "Germany First" principle.
▽ Triumphant Japan shatters the A.B.D.A. front in the East Indies.

> ▷ *Japanese troops land from their transports. The Allied naval forces in the Dutch East Indies were powerless to stop the Japanese "leap-frog" advance to the south.*
> ▽ *Japanese paratroops go in to establish yet another foot-hold during the fight for the Dutch East Indies.*

would then be available for active operations.

It was maintained among General Douglas MacArthur's staff that this decision had been wrung from Roosevelt by Churchill's plausible eloquence. This was not in fact so; the American Chiefs-of-Staff, quite independently of the British and for purely national reasons, were already entirely in favour of the "Germany first" principle. However, it must be noted that in his memoirs MacArthur, the defender of the Philippines, claims that he was kept in ignorance of this important decision, and it is understandable that as a result of this omission he remained somewhat bitter against Marshall.

On the other hand, no great importance need be attached to the criticism MacArthur made of Admiral King, the new Chief of Naval Operations, when he wrote:

"Although Admiral King felt that the fleet did not have sufficient resources to proceed to Manila, it was my impression that our Navy depreciated its own strength and might well have cut through to relieve our hard-pressed forces. The Japanese blockade of the Philippines was to some extent a paper blockade. Mindanao was still accessible and firmly held by us. The bulk of the Japanese Navy, operating on tight schedules, was headed south for the seizure of Borneo, Malaya and Indonesia. American carriers having escaped destruction at Pearl Harbor could have approached the Philippines and unloaded planes on fields in Mindanao."

Writing about Pearl Harbor shortly before his death in 1966, Admiral Chester W. Nimitz, who must share with MacArthur the credit for the final defeat of Japan, said:

"No one regrets more than I our 3,000 dead when the Japanese attacked Pearl Harbor. But if Admiral Husband Kimmel, who at that time commanded the American forces at Pearl Harbor, had had information of the attack 24 hours in advance, he would have sent off all our forces to meet the Japanese.

"We had not one aircraft-carrier capable of opposing Admiral Nagumo's aircraft-carrier formation, and the Japanese would have sunk all our ships on the high seas.

"We would have lost 6,000 men and almost all our Pacific Fleet."

This was the position on the day of the attack. But on the next day, when the aircraft-carriers *Lexington* and *Enterprise* reached Pearl Harbor, there was no question of sending them out on an operation against six other carriers without the advantage of surprise. Moreover, the six aircraft-carriers of the Japanese striking force each carried at least 60 planes, all superior in performance to the 80 machines on each of the American carriers.

MacArthur's proposed operation would therefore in all probability have led to a second Pearl Harbor, but this time in mid-ocean, with no hope of rescue.

Joint efforts in South-East Asia

Faced with Japanese aggression that had been prepared and worked out at leisure, the "Arcadia" Conference hastily formed the A.B.D.A. command, the initials standing for the American, British, Dutch, and Australian forces fighting the Japanese in the Philippines, Malaya, Burma, and the Dutch East Indies. The establishment and appointments for this unified command, which Churchill cheerfully compared with Marshal Foch's appointment as Allied generalissimo on March 26, 1918, gave rise to hard talking among the conference delegates at the White House.

The Americans wanted the commander-in-chief to be British and expressed a preference for Sir Archibald Wavell; the British refused to accept any responsibility for this, giving somewhat unconvincing reasons for their hesitation.

Though Churchill remained optimistic about the fate of Singapore, Sir John Dill, in a letter to Sir Alan Brooke, introducing him to his new duties as C.I.G.S., gave his views on the subject and put forward an argument, which he could obviously not pursue at an inter-Allied conference. He wrote, not mincing his words:

"It would, I think, be fatal to have a British commander responsible for the disasters that are coming to the Americans as well as ourselves ... Never was a soldier given a more difficult task ... It is of the first importance that we should not be blamed for the bloody noses that are coming to them."

However, General Marshall and President Roosevelt carried the day, with the result that on January 15, 1942, General Wavell started to set up his A.B.D.A. headquarters at Batavia. He was assigned three deputy commanders: General H. ter Poorten, a Dutch officer, for the land forces; Admiral Thomas Hart, C.-in-C. U.S. Asiatic Fleet, for the naval forces; and Air-Marshal Sir Richard Peirse for the air forces. Although the command struc-

▽ *The victory march through Malaya: a Japanese infantry column, complete with flag, fords a creek. The British strategy of defending the key roads and relying on jungle and swamp to guard their flanks was foiled by the skill shown by the Japanese at jungle infiltration. They found, for example, that "impassable" mangrove swamps can be crossed by treading on the roots of the trees, and they bypassed the British positions time and again.*

ture appeared logical and workable, Wavell, seeing that the *matériel* resources of his command were poor and obsolete, noted sarcastically: "I had been handed not just a baby but quadruplets."

Malaya in danger

The Japanese offensive, making full use of its considerable *matériel* superiority, particularly at sea and in the air, was now in full spate, with its right wing threatening Burma and its left Australia. Success followed success.

Lieutenant-General A. E. Percival, G.O.C. Malaya, had III Indian Corps with which to try to oppose the Japanese advance. This corps, under the command of Lieutenant-General Sir Lewis Heath, disposed of three divisions, the 9th and 11th Indian in the line and the 8th Australian in reserve. Percival, faced with the problem of defending the Malay Peninsula, at places 175 miles wide, was forced to deploy his forces to cover the main axial roads, while the Japanese, with four, and later five, divisions, either infiltrated the British line through the jungle or bypassed the British positions by carrying out amphibious landings in their rear.

British weaknesses

The British dispositions left much to be desired, and this, combined with their numerical inferiority, meant that they could not halt the Japanese thrusts. Moreover, the naval and air forces could not concentrate on the actions in the north, for they also had to cover convoys making for Singapore via the Sunda Strait rather than the Malacca Strait, as the latter was now threatened by the Japanese. These convoys did, however, bring in useful reinforcements: an Indian brigade on January 3, the 53rd Brigade of the 18th Division from Britain on the 13th, a second Indian brigade on the 22nd, and the rest of the 18th Division on the 29th. But the training of the Indian troops was entirely inadequate, and the British division, which had originally been intended for the Middle East and diverted to Malaya at the Cape of Good Hope, had declined in efficiency during its long sea passage.

◁ ◁ *Manning the landing-craft during the invasion of North Borneo—a painting by the Japanese artist Toyoshiro Fukuda. The first landings on Borneo went in as early as December 17, long before the Philippines had been secured.*
◁ *Japanese infantry double forwards to the attack.*
▽ *A scene during the furious battle for Kuala Lumpur in Malaya. The town finally fell to the Japanese on January 11.*

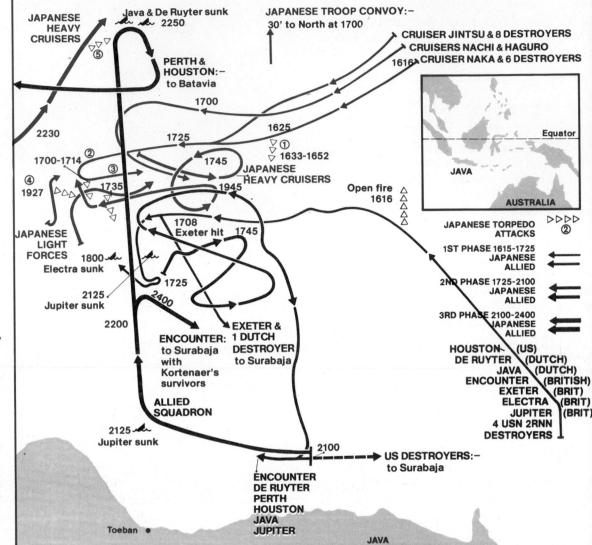

JAPANESE HEAVY CRUISERS

Java & De Ruyter sunk
2250

JAPANESE TROOP CONVOY:–
30' to North at 1700

CRUISER JINTSU & 8 DESTROYERS
CRUISERS NACHI & HAGURO
1616 CRUISER NAKA & 6 DESTROYERS

PERTH & HOUSTON:–
to Batavia

1700

2230

1725

1625

1700-1714 ②

③

1745

JAPANESE HEAVY CRUISERS

④
1927

1735

1945

① 1633-1652

Open fire
1616

1708
Exeter hit

1745

Equator

JAVA

AUSTRALIA

JAPANESE LIGHT FORCES

Electra sunk

1800

1725

2125
Jupiter sunk

2400

2200

ENCOUNTER:
to Surabaja
with
Kortenaer's
survivors

EXETER &
1 DUTCH
DESTROYER
to Surabaja

JAPANESE TORPEDO ATTACKS   ②

1ST PHASE 1615-1725
JAPANESE
ALLIED

2ND PHASE 1725-2100
JAPANESE
ALLIED

3RD PHASE 2100-2400
JAPANESE
ALLIED

HOUSTON   (US)
DE RUYTER   (DUTCH)
JAVA   (DUTCH)
ENCOUNTER   (BRITISH)
EXETER   (BRIT)
ELECTRA   (BRIT)
JUPITER   (BRIT)
4 USN 2RNN
DESTROYERS

ALLIED SQUADRON

2125
Jupiter sunk

2100

US DESTROYERS:–
to Surabaja

ENCOUNTER
DE RUYTER
PERTH
HOUSTON
JAVA
JUPITER

Toeban ●

JAVA

▷ *The Battle of the Java Sea, in which the last Allied attempt to counter the Japanese invasion of Java was broken. Rear-Admiral Karel Doorman of the Royal Netherlands Navy sailed with an ill-assorted American-British-Dutch-Australian squadron to intercept and destroy the Japanese invasion convoy, but his force was relentlessly ground down and destroyed by the covering Japanese cruiser squadrons.*

▽ *Poster for the Free Dutch Navy. The units of the Dutch Navy stationed in the Far East fought gallantly beside their allies; but the sheer speed of the Japanese advance meant that the multi-national naval forces defending the "Malay Barrier" never had the time to learn how to manoeuvre and fight at maximum efficiency.*

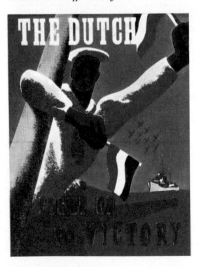

The new Japanese objectives

Meanwhile, the Japanese Navy had also been moving forward, stretching out its tentacles to seize the bases it coveted, as Admiral Morison puts it. These tentacles consisted of the 2nd Scouting Fleet, 3rd Blockade and Transport Fleet, and 4th Mandate Fleet. The 2nd Scouting Fleet, commanded by Vice-Admiral Kondo, was to assist in the capture of Malaya and the reduction of the "impregnable" fortress of Singapore; the 3rd Blockade and Transport Fleet, under Vice-Admiral Takahashi, was ordered to gain possession of the Philippines, Borneo, and Celebes and then to join forces with the 2nd Scouting Fleet in order to take the Dutch East Indies, with their coveted oilfields; and the 4th Mandate Fleet,

commanded by Vice-Admiral Inouye, was to take Guam and Wake. The attainment of these objectives would secure the perimeter of the Greater South-East Asia Co-Prosperity Sphere.

It should also be noted here that the Japanese land-based air forces co-operated very efficiently with the 2nd and 3rd Fleets, which had no carriers. From December 15, 1941 they operated from the base at Davao on the island of Mindanao; Kendari airfield, in the south of Celebes, was captured in record time on January 17 and was soon in full swing as a Japanese advanced base; Amboina, in the Moluccas, was captured on February 3. From these bases, the Japanese could wreak havoc over the whole area of operations assigned to the 2nd and 3rd Fleets.

Besides being better trained than the Allied pilots opposing them, the Japanese had a distinct advantage in numbers and *matériel*. Most of the Hawker Hurricanes which had reached Singapore on January

4 were quickly overwhelmed in the air or destroyed on the ground, and a second consignment of these fighters, the only Allied aircraft in the theatre capable of taking on the Zero at anything like even terms, was diverted to Java. And thus the Japanese bombers had a field day at little cost. On February 3, Surabaja in Java was bombed for the first time; the next day the American cruisers *Houston* and *Marblehead* were both hit, the second badly enough to have to return to Australia for repairs.

Borneo and Sumatra Invaded

The first Japanese landing on Borneo occurred at Miri, on December 16. The oil port of Tarakan, near the entrance to the Makassar Strait, and Manado, at the northern tip of Celebes, both fell on the same day, January 11, 1942. During the night of January 24, a division of American destroyers surprised the Japanese as they were landing an invasion force at Balikpapan, where most of Borneo's oil was refined, and sank four merchantmen, but this success could not alter the course of events. Without even taking into account the fall of Kendari and Amboina, or waiting for the capture of Singapore, the Japanese invaded Sumatra, on February 14, and Timor on the 20th, without making any distinction between the Portuguese and Dutch parts of the island. This advance was of great strategic import, as it breached the "Malay barrier" and thus gave the Japanese the opportunity of cutting communications with Australia.

The situation was now beyond any hope of remedy, and on February 25 Wavell received orders to move his headquarters back to Ceylon, to which he had been preceded, on February 14, by Admiral

△ *The whirling chaos of an air/sea battle, captured by a Japanese artist. In the Java Sea campaign the Japanese did not need Nagumo's carriers. Land-based aircraft gave them virtually unchallenged air superiority.*

△ *A column of Japanese tanks rumbles across the Causeway from the mainland to Singapore Island.*

Hart. Command of the Allied naval forces still operating against the Japanese had devolved upon the Dutch Vice-Admiral C. E. L. Helfrich, who was later to show exceptional courage in a disastrous situation.

Battle of the Java Sea

Meanwhile, the Allied advanced headquarters at Bandung in Java had received information that two convoys, totalling 97 transports and with powerful escorts, had been observed off the Malay Peninsula and leaving the Makassar Strait. These were in fact the convoys carrying the Japanese 16th Army to the invasion of Java. With three divisions and one brigade, this force was far superior to the 30,000 trained troops with which General

ter Poorten had to conduct the defence of Java.

Java's only hope lay in the destruction of the two convoys before they reached the island. To this end, the Allied naval forces in the area were dispatched under the Dutch Rear-Admiral Karel Doorman to the decisive Battle of the Java Sea. The Allied force, however, was at a distinct disadvantage as it had not had the time to learn to co-ordinate its efforts properly and to work out a common signalling code. Doorman's command consisted of two heavy cruisers, the British *Exeter* and American *Houston*; three light cruisers, the Dutch *De Ruyter* and *Java*, and the Australian *Perth*; and nine destroyers, four American, three British, and two Dutch.

On February 27, at 1500, Doorman was at sea off Surabaja when he received orders to intercept the Japanese convoy heading from the Makassar Strait towards Surabaja. Contact was made at about 1615 between the Allied force and the Japanese escort under Rear-Admiral Nishimura: the heavy cruisers *Nachi* (Rear-Admiral Takagi) and *Haguro*, the light cruisers *Naka* (Nishimura) and *Jintsu*, and 13 destroyers.

Though the Allies thus had a numerical superiority in cruisers, the range at which the action opened, more than 13 miles, meant that it was the numbers of 8-inch guns involved that was the critical factor. And here the Japanese prevailed, with 20 such weapons against the Allies' 12 (it should be remembered that *Houston* had been hit by bombs on February 4, and this had knocked out her aftermost turret). The battle was to continue for almost seven hours without achieving concrete results, partly because the Japanese were more concerned with the safety of their convoy than sinking Allied vessels, and partly because the Allied warships had no reconnaissance aircraft, and were thus forced, as Morison puts it, to play a kind of blind man's bluff.

During the first engagement, *Exeter* was hit in her engine room at 1708 and hauled out of the line, the cruisers following her doing the same under the impression that such a manoeuvre had been ordered by Doorman in *De Ruyter*, leading the Allied line. While the crippled British cruiser made for Surabaja, the Japanese launched a wave of 72 torpedoes, only one of which, remarkably, hit an Allied warship, the Dutch destroyer *Kortenaer*, which exploded and sank. While covering

The Japanese Type 95 "KYUGO" light tank

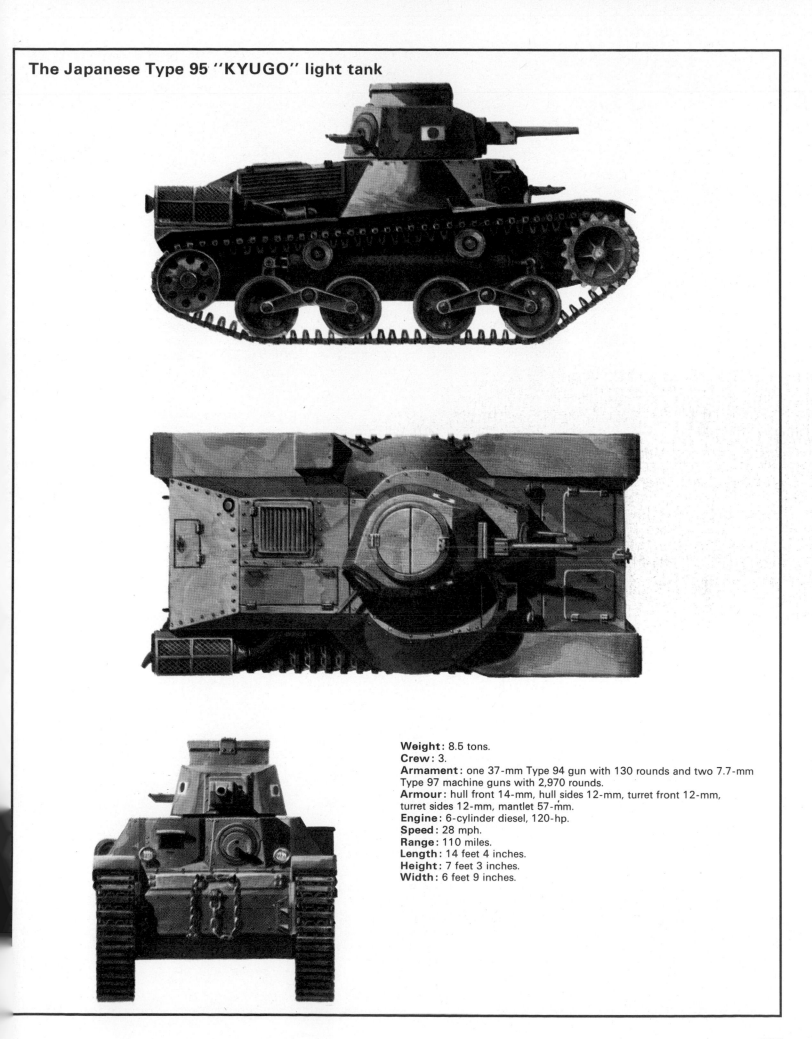

Weight: 8.5 tons.
Crew: 3.
Armament: one 37-mm Type 94 gun with 130 rounds and two 7.7-mm Type 97 machine guns with 2,970 rounds.
Armour: hull front 14-mm, hull sides 12-mm, turret front 12-mm, turret sides 12-mm, mantlet 57-mm.
Engine: 6-cylinder diesel, 120-hp.
Speed: 28 mph.
Range: 110 miles.
Length: 14 feet 4 inches.
Height: 7 feet 3 inches.
Width: 6 feet 9 inches.

How they surrendered:

"Answer me briefly. Do you wish to surrender unconditionally?" "Yes we do." "Have you any Japanese prisoners of war?" "None at all." "Have you any Japanese civilians?" "No. They have all been sent to India." "Very well. You will please sign this document of surrender."

Percival read about half of it and then asked: "Would you wait until tomorrow morning?" Yamashita replied angrily: "If you don't sign now we shall go on fighting. All I want to know is: Do you surrender unconditionally or not?" Percival went pale and began talking to the interpreter in a low voice, but Yamashita interrupted him, pointed his finger and shouted "Yes or no?" Percival glanced towards the interpreter, then said "Yes." "Very well. We shall cease hostilities at 10 pm, Japanese time."

the retirement of *Exeter*, the British destroyer *Electra* was stopped by gunfire and hammered into a blazing wreck. During the night, Doorman searched in vain for the Japanese convoy, which had been ordered by Nishimura to retreat to the north during the action, without finding it. He was also forced to release his American destroyers, which had expended all their torpedoes and were running drastically short of fuel.

During his fruitless search for the Japanese transports, however, Doorman once again ran into their escort, in the form of the cruiser *Jintsu* and her seven destroyers, at 1930. Turning away from the Japanese cruiser, Doorman inadvertently led his force over a newly-laid Dutch minefield, which cost him the British destroyer *Jupiter*. But time was running out for the Allied ships, for Japanese seaplanes had been keeping their cruisers informed of the Allied survivors' movements, and *Nachi* and *Haguro* were moving in for the kill. During the subsequent engagement, *De Ruyter* and *Java* were both hit and sunk by Japanese torpedoes. Doorman went down with his flagship. Immediately afterwards *Perth* and *Houston* broke off the action and returned to Batavia.

The crisis in Allied naval fortunes had yet further to run, however. After re-fuelling at Batavia, *Perth* and *Houston* received orders to retire southwards through the Sunda Strait. Here they ran into the second of the Japanese convoys mentioned above. This had sailed from Indo-China and was in the process of landing the first units of the Japanese 2nd Division in Banten Bay. The two Allied cruisers immediately went into the attack, and managed to sink one transport and force three others to beach themselves, as well as damaging one cruiser and three destroyers, before being sunk by the rest of the Japanese escort.

A few hours later, *Exeter* sailed from Surabaja with two destroyers to try to pass through the Sunda Strait. They were spotted by Japanese reconnaissance aircraft and sunk by four cruisers and three destroyers on March 1.

Defeat in Java

The naval defeat of February 27 sealed the fate of Java. The two vital centres of Batavia and Surabaja fell into Imamura's

hands, and General ter Poorten asked the Japanese commander for armistice terms. As was to be expected, the victor demanded unconditional surrender, which he received at Bandung on March 10. Sherwood notes at this time:

"Churchill, who had won his greatest Parliamentary triumph a scant three weeks before, now faced the worst predicament of his career as Prime Minister. He made a broadcast speech in which he attributed the whole series of misfortunes in the Far East to the fact that America's shield of sea power had been 'dashed to the ground' at Pearl Harbor. There were

numerous expressions of irritation at this statement in Washington, as though Churchill were attempting to escape censure by blaming it all on the U.S. Navy, but it did not bother Roosevelt at all. He merely remarked: 'Winston had to say *something*."

Retreat to Singapore

Under the keen and vigorous command of Lieutenant-General Tomoyuki Yamashita, the Japanese 25th Army smashed its way through the British defences in the north of Malaya. On January 1, 1942 Kuantan, on the east coast, fell to the swiftly-advancing Japanese, while on the other side of the country Kuala Lumpur, on the Slim river, succumbed on the 11th, after a period of fierce resistance. Seeing

◁△ *With further resistance on Singapore Island impossible, General Percival (far right of group) marches out to sign the agreement for the surrender of the garrison.*
◁▽ *Victor and vanquished: a belligerent Yamashita faces Percival across the conference table and tells him that unless unconditional surrender is agreed to promptly the Japanese forces will resume hostilities.*

△ *Japanese troops march into surrendered Singapore.*

his reserves melting away, Percival ordered his forces to fall back on Singapore on January 29, after asking for and receiving Wavell's authorisation. On January 30 the causeway linking the island fortress and the mainland was blown up.

But Singapore's garrison, its back to the wall, was in no position to offer a solid resistance for the great imperial base, which was intended to close the Indian Ocean to attack from the east and to ensure the safety of Britain's sea link with Australia and New Zealand. The politico-military squabbles between the wars, which had resulted in the island's impoverished defences, are too complex to be treated here, but had provided Singapore with adequate defences against attack from the sea: the southern shore was provided with numerous batteries of guns, including two with five 15-inch pieces. The land front had been neglected, however, as it had been thought impossible for an enemy to attack Singapore via the thick jungles of Malaya.

In his memoirs, Churchill tells us of the

▷ *The "Tiger of Malaya"– General Yamashita, a tough, thrusting commander who brooked no delay to his lightning campaign in Malaya and Singapore.*
▽ *British prisoners in Singapore await their transfer to prison camp–first in the comparative comfort of Changi Jail, but later, for thousands, amid the horrors of the "Death Railway" in Siam.*

"feelings of painful surprise" he had when reading Wavell's message of January 16, which emphasised this failing in the Singapore position. Churchill adds:

"Moreover, even more astounding, no measures worth speaking of had been taken by any of the commanders since the war began, and more especially since the Japanese had established themselves in Indo-China, to construct field defences. They had not even mentioned the fact they did not exist." But Churchill, who was also his own Minister of Defence, was not in the habit of making others bear responsibilities that were his. He sums up as follows:

"I do not write this in any way to excuse myself. I ought to have known. My advisers ought to have known and I ought to have been told, and ought to have asked. The reason I had not asked about this matter, amid the thousands of questions I put, was that the possibility of Singapore having no landward defences no more entered into my mind than that of a battleship being launched without a bottom."

The fall of Singapore

In the circumstances, it was not difficult for General Yamashita, on the night of February 8–9, to get his forces across the Strait of Johore and win a beach-head north-west of the city of Singapore. Immediately afterwards, the Japanese captured Tengah airfield and the reservoirs supplying the city's million inhabitants with water.

On February 15, the advanced guard of the Japanese 5th Division ran into the British delegation sent out to seek terms for surrender. General Yamashita refused to discuss terms, but insisted that General Percival come to see him personally. The Japanese commander told Percival that his forces "respect the valour of your army and will honour your dead", but then insisted on unconditional surrender. Percival hesitated for nearly an hour, and then signed the British surrender.

One of Yamashita's staff then asked if he was to prepare for a victory parade through the streets of Singapore, to which he received the dry reply:

"No. The war isn't finished. We have lost 3,300 men in the campaign. What have the survivors done to deserve it? We must first honour our dead. Then we'll prepare for future campaigns."

The disaster in Malaya provoked another crisis between the irritable Mr. Curtin and Churchill, following on their earlier disagreement about Tobruk.

Curtin had a majority of two in the Australian parliament and stubbornly refused to introduce the conscription necessary for the defence of Australia. This did not, however, prevent him from abusing Churchill for his lack of zeal in calling the home country to the defence of her Pacific dominions. On December 27, 1941, for example, the following virtual ultimatum appeared over Curtin's signature in the *Melbourne Herald*:

"Without any inhibitions of any kind, I make it quite clear that Australia looks to America, free of any pangs as to our traditional links with the United Kingdom.

"We know the problems that the United Kingdom faces. We know the constant threat of invasion. We know the dangers of dispersal of strength. But we know too that Australia can go, and Britain can still hold on.

"We are therefore determined that Australia shall not go, and we shall exert all our energies towards the shaping of a plan, with the United States as its keystone, which will give to our country some confidence of being able to hold out until the tide of battle swings against the enemy.

"Summed up, Australian external policy will be shaped towards obtaining Russian aid, and working out, with the United States, as the major factor, a plan of Pacific strategy, along with British, Chinese, and Dutch forces."

The reader will be spared the details of the somewhat acrimonious correspondence which followed. In the course of this the Australian Prime Minister went so far as to inform his British opposite number that after all the assurances that had been given to various Canberra governments for years: "the evacuation of Singapore would be regarded here and elsewhere as an inexcusable betrayal."

But it must be emphasised that Churchill, for all his normal impetuosity, made no attempt to modify his attitude to placate the Australian Prime Minister. Faced with the daily-growing threat of the Japanese advance, it was decided to withdraw the 6th and 7th Australian Divisions from the Middle East and incorporate them into the defence of Java and what British and American strategists called the "Malay barrier", separating the Indian Ocean from the Pacific.

△ *Berlin's* Lustige Blätter *jibes at Anglo-Australian discord. "This blighter's really getting me down," grumbles the Australian kangaroo; "I'll have to kick him out."*

▽ Travaso *of Rome salutes the new conquests of Italy's Japanese partner: "Delicacies of the season— yellow sweetbreads."*

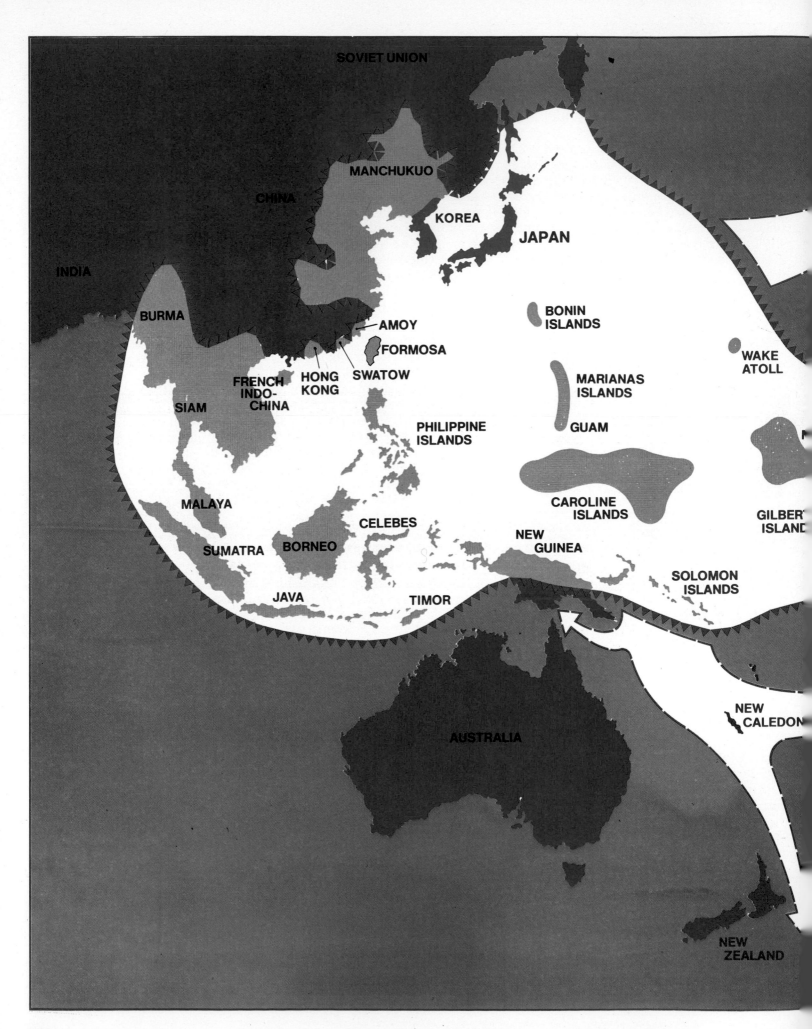

SOVIET UNION

CHINA

MANCHUKUO

KOREA

JAPAN

INDIA

BURMA

AMOY

BONIN
ISLANDS

FORMOSA

WAKE
ATOLL

FRENCH
INDO-
CHINA

HONG
KONG

SWATOW

MARIANAS
ISLANDS

SIAM

GUAM

PHILIPPINE
ISLANDS

MALAYA

CELEBES

CAROLINE
ISLANDS

GILBER'
ISLAND

SUMATRA

BORNEO

NEW
GUINEA

SOLOMON
ISLANDS

JAVA

TIMOR

NEW
CALEDON

AUSTRALIA

NEW
ZEALAND

798

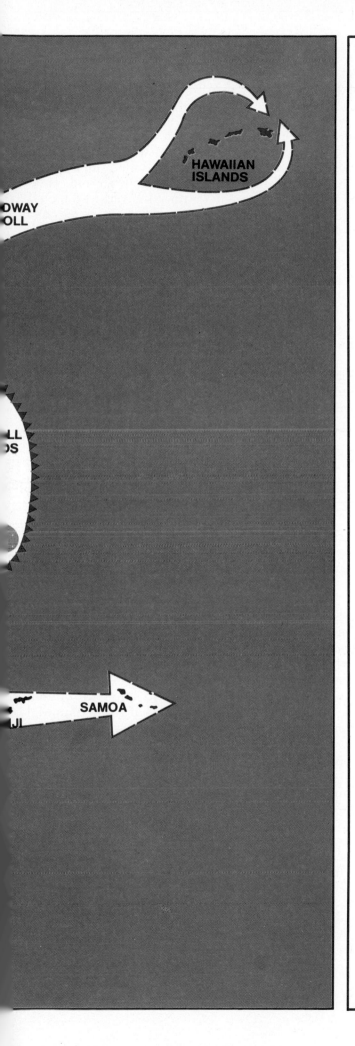

HAWAIIAN
ISLANDS

DWAY
OLL

LL
DS

SAMOA

JI

A new ailment: "Victory Disease"

"Victory Disease" was the term coined by the Japanese
themselves to describe the over-confidence which led
them to take on too much with too little. Like the
Germans in Russia, they found that their initial
successes gave them an extended front which was one
long salient, and salients are as vulnerable to enemy
counter-attacks as they are helpful to expansion. When
transplanted into the realities of the Pacific war,
however, this meant considerably more problems for
the Japanese than they had had at the beginning of the
war. Theirs was not a continuous land front but an
invisible perimeter: dots of land interspersed with
thousands of miles of open sea. And the outermost
islands under Japanese control were uncomfortably
close to others under Allied control.

What the Japanese strategists found, after the first
intoxicating run of victories, was that there were
a lot of loose ends still to be tied up. To the south-
east, the Allies were still holding on in southern
New Guinea, stalling the effective isolation of Australia
from the United States. To the East, the Americans were
still established on Midway Atoll, the western
extremity of the Hawaiian chain. If New Guinea–and
with it New Caledonia, Fiji, and Samoa–could be added
to the list of Japanese conquests, not only Australia
but New Zealand could be cut off. If Midway could be
taken, the Hawaiian Islands themselves, and the all-
important Pearl Harbor naval base, could later be
reduced in turn, which would push the Americans right
back to the Pacific coast of the United States.

None of these new objectives had formed part of the
initial plan, which had centred on the reduction of the
"Southern Area": the Philippines, Malaya, and the East
Indies. This was to have been followed by a period of
consolidation. But the ease with which the first
objectives were gained led the Japanese High Command
to formulate new plans which would keep up the
pressure while the going was good. Draft plans were
prepared for the New Guinea–Samoa drive and the
pounce on Midway which, it was expected, would
finally extend to Pearl Harbor.

In purely logical terms, the confidence with which the
Japanese turned to these ambitious new projects can be
explained easily enough. After all, the entire scope of
the "Southern Area" campaign had been no less
ambitious, and the result had been as overwhelmingly
successful as it was economical. But the new plans
meant expanding from an already expanded perimeter,
using forces which were already widely dispersed and
must now be dispersed still more. And unless the Allied
forces still resisting in the Pacific were totally destroyed
this time, even partial failure would give Japan nothing
more than thousands more miles of vulnerable flank. It
was the refusal to consider the latter–failure, even
partial failure–which was the worst symptom of
"Victory Disease".

CHAPTER 59
Bataan & Corregidor

△ Simplicissimus *of Munich lampoons MacArthur's discomfiture on Bataan. "Mirror, mirror on the wall; who's the greatest general in the land?" You, of course–but Wavell's more skilful!"*
▷ *The end on Bataan–American and Filipino troops surrender.*

Meanwhile, the defence of the Philippines had been concentrated in the Bataan Peninsula, west of Manila Bay. Here MacArthur had 15,000 Americans and 65,000 Filipinos, although only 10,000 of the latter could be considered as fully trained soldiers. MacArthur's foresight had provided the garrison with ample ammunition, but the position with food supplies was a problem right from the beginning of the siege as the provisions for the garrison itself had to be spread to feed the thousands of refugees who had fled the Japanese advance and now seriously jeopardised the defence of Bataan. Notwithstanding, the American and Filipino forces on the peninsula held out for a very creditable period, not surrendering until April 9, 1942 after a siege of 98 days.

Bataan holds out

On January 10, Lieutenant-General Homma, the commander of the Japanese 14th Army, sent the following message to MacArthur:

"Sir,

You are well aware that you are doomed. The end is near. The question is how long you will be able to resist. You have already cut rations by half. I appreciate the fighting spirit of yourself and your troops who have been fighting with courage. Your prestige and honour have been upheld.

"However, in order to avoid needless bloodshed and to save the remnants of your divisions and your auxiliary troops, you are advised to surrender."

When this summons remained unanswered, the 14th Army attacked the American lines during the night of the 11th. After ten days of fruitless frontal attacks, the Japanese infiltrated the American lines across the slopes of Mount Natib, which the defenders had thought inaccessible, and thus forced the Americans to fall back to their second defence line across the peninsula. The retreat was conducted in an orderly fashion, however, and the American forces did not lose their cohesion. Homma, to his extreme chagrin, had to ask Tokyo for reinforcements.

On February 22, MacArthur received a message from the White House ordering him to quit Bataan, organise the defence of Mindanao to the south, and then proceed to Australia. MacArthur delayed in executing these orders, claiming that his departure would result in the immediate collapse of resistance in the Philippines. On March 10, however, Roosevelt cabled him: "Proceed immediately to Melbourne." General MacArthur could no longer ignore this direct order, and on the night of the 11th, he and his staff sailed from his command post on the island of Corregidor in four PT boats (motor torpedo boats). After an eventful three days at sea, MacArthur landed at Cagayan de Oro in Mindanao, flying from there to Australia on board a B-17 bomber. On this occasion he made his celebrated promise to the journalists waiting for him: "I shall return!"

Major-General J. M. Wainwright, who succeeded MacArthur as commander in the Philippines, visited his superior just before he left. Their conversation has been preserved by John Toland:

"' Jonathan,' [MacArthur] said as they shook hands, 'I want you to understand my position very plainly.' He was leaving he said, only because of insistent, repeated orders from Roosevelt. At first he had told his staff he would refuse, but they convinced him that defying the President's direct order would bring disciplinary action. 'I want you to make it known throughout all elements of your command that I'm leaving over my repeated protests.'

"'Of course I will, Douglas,' said Wainwright.

"'If I get through to Australia, you know I'll come back as soon as I can with as much as I can.' Then he warned of the necessity of greater defense in depth. 'And be sure to give them everything you've got with your artillery. That's the best arm you have.'

"The two men were quiet for a moment. In the distance the dull rumble of battle from Bataan could be heard. Wainwright was thinking of the dwindling ammunition and food supply, his air force of two battered P-40's, of the spreading malaria and dysentery and lack of medicine. He

△ *One of the last discussions between Wainright and MacArthur (right) before the latter handed over the defence of Bataan and set off for Australia. MacArthur's famous promise "I will return" was fulfilled in time–but years too late for the defenders of Bataan.*

▽ *MacArthur's triumphant arrival in Australia after an eventful voyage by PT boat. After the traumatic experience of the Philippine campaign, it was hardly surprising that he became the champion of all Allied ventures intended to bring the war home to Japan rather than to Germany or Italy.*

said, 'You'll get through.'

"'And back,' MacArthur added with determination. He gave Wainwright a box of cigars and two large jars of shaving cream. 'Good-bye Jonathan.' They shook hands warmly. 'If you're still on Bataan when I get back, I'll make you a Lieutenant-General.'

"'I'll be on Bataan if I'm still alive.' Wainwright turned and slowly started back to his lunch."

MacArthur: the right man?

Lieutenant-General Douglas MacArthur had a strong and somewhat theatrical personality. He was the object of passionate disagreement in his own country, not only in political circles, where he was regarded as a possible rival to Roosevelt, but also among his peers in the army and navy, among whom aroused feelings of great admiration or great animosity. To describe him we may quote the evidence of a British officer who was far from indulgent when assessing the great American military commanders. On leaving Tokyo on November 22, 1945, where he had visited MacArthur, Lord Alanbrooke noted in his diary:

"MacArthur was the greatest general and best strategist that the war produced. He certainly outshone Marshall, Eisenhower and all the other American and British generals including Montgomery. As a fighter of battles and as a leader of men Montgomery was hard to beat, but I doubt whether he could have shown the same strategic genius had he been in MacArthur's position."

Alanbrooke believed that MacArthur, apart from his outstanding qualities as a war leader, also showed great political and diplomatic ability, and this view may certainly be correct. In fact, MacArthur succeeded in keeping the loyalty of the Filipinos during the Japanese occupation, remained on good terms with the intractable Curtin, and after the war won the friendship of Emperor Hirohito and helped the Japanese get over their defeat.

Surrender on Bataan

When he arrived in Australia, General MacArthur, who had been eating at the same mess as his men, noted that he had lost nearly two stones in weight at Bataan. It is thus clear that the American garrison was severely weakened when Homma launched his final assault. Added to this physical debilitation was the loss of morale of the troops, to whom it was now abundantly clear that there was no possibility of a relief force reaching them. These facts, then, make it clear why General Wainwright was unable to galvanise his men to action. Moreover, the Japanese 14th Army had been reinforced with another division and brigade, and had improved its tactics, from now on combining frontal assaults with small-scale landings in the Americans' rear.

On April 1 Wainwright ignored a fresh summons from Homma to surrender and accept an "honourable defeat". The final Japanese attack started two days later, and three days after that the American defences were finally breached. After the failure of one counter-attack, General King, commanding on Bataan, considered that his men were at the end of their tether and sent emissaries to the Japanese to discuss terms on April 9. The surrender was signed the next day; 64,000 Filipinos and 12,000 Americans were taken prisoner.

The Bataan "Death March"

There then followed the notorious "Death March", when the prisoners taken on Bataan were marched from Mariveles 55 miles to the railhead at San Fernando, under the most inhuman conditions. During the march, 2,330 Americans and between 7–10,000 Filipinos died. As the officer responsible, General Homma was tried after the war, found guilty, and executed. General MacArthur, turning down a final appeal for Homma, said: "I am again confronted with the repugnant duty of passing final judgement on a former adversary in a major military campaign ... I approve the finding of guilt and direct the Commanding General, United States Forces in the Western Pacific to execute the sentence."

But the American historian John Toland examined all the documents pertaining to the case and did not come to such definite conclusions about Homma's guilt, attaching blame more to the 14th Army's general staff for their irresponsibility than to Homma himself for criminal intent. The Japanese had expected to find 30,000 prisoners and got 76,000, all of them in poor physical condition. Twenty miles from Mariveles, transport had been provided for the rest of the journey, but only 230 trucks were available. Moreover, the behaviour of the Japanese guards towards their prisoners varied considerably: in some cases it was relatively humane, in others completely abominable. This seems to indicate that these guards were not obeying a general directive from their superiors.

The end in the Philippines

The Japanese now controlled all of Luzon except the island fortress of Corregidor and the islets surrounding it. While the Americans held these, the Japanese were denied the use of Manila harbour. On May 4, the Japanese poured a barrage of 16,000 shells onto the island, and under the cover so provided landed a powerful assault force, which managed to secure a small beach-head. The American garrison numbered 15,000, but of these only 1,300 could be considered battleworthy. Homma

urged Wainwright to surrender, but insisted that if he did so, the capitulation must also apply to all other American forces in the Philippines archipelago. The Japanese would thus be able to secure Mindanao and the islands around the Visayan Sea without firing a shot.

▽ *With his assault forces safely established ashore, General Homma lands on Luzon.*
▽▽ *The Japanese did not have things all their own way in the Philippines, witness these Japanese prisoners taken in an over-confident attack.*

803

△ *"Toul Pocket, Bataan" by
Stanley Dersh. The painting
depicts the desperate American-
Filipino counter-attack in mid-
February 1942 which wiped out
the Japanese salients pushed
into the American front and
postponed the struggle on Bataan
for another two months. (This
painting was later used for
propaganda purposes on a U.S.
Department of the Army poster.)*

After a painful mental struggle, and
despite MacArthur's intervention, Wainwright finally ordered his subordinates to
terminate their resistance. The latter at
first protested, but all American resistance
finally ended on May 6, 1942. Wainwright
was not condemned for ordering the
capitulation by the American Government, General Marshall, and MacArthur.
Indeed, with General Percival, who had
surrendered Singapore, he was one of
those invited to the Japanese surrender
ceremony on September 2, 1945.

The turn of Burma

According to Churchill, it was not expected in London that the Japanese would
invade Burma until they had finished with
Malaya and conquered Singapore. As a
result of this lack of foresight, the defences
of this wealthy colony were extremely
sparse. On December 8, 1941 they com-

prised troops totalling about a division –
the 1st Burma Division, Burmese battalions stiffened by two British battalions
and an Indian brigade. Towards the end
of January 1942, the incomplete 17th
Indian Division was shipped in. The whole
was under Major-General T. J. Hutton.
The R.A.F. was in an even worse position,
with only four Bristol Blenheim light
bombers and 32 superannuated Brewster
Buffalo fighters, of which only 24 were
airworthy.

Burma was as important to the Japanese
as Malaya or India, not only for its oil and
other natural resources, but because it
contained the "Burma Road", which had
only recently been completed and linked
Lashio in Burma with Chungking in
China. As President Roosevelt had just
extended Lend-Lease to Nationalist
China, the Japanese High Command
considered it vital to sever this only artery
supplying Generalissimo Chiang Kai-
shek's forces with war supplies from the
"arsenal of democracy". The task of

destroying this link was entrusted to the 15th Army, under Lieutenant-General S. Iida.

The invaders also had aid in Burma in the form of a large number of agents, whom the Japanese had been enlisting for years. The British knew of this, and on January 18, 1942 arrested the Prime Minister, U Saw. On the same day the Japanese 15th Army took the port and airfield of Tavoy in the south and moved on Moulmein, at the mouth of the Salween. This river, which formed a considerable natural barrier, did not slow the Japanese for long. Moulmein fell on the 31st, and the Japanese pushed on towards the Sittang. The critical phase of the campaign was reached when the Japanese arrived at this river before the retreating 17th Indian Division, under the command of Major-General J. Smyth, V.C. The bridge the division was to have used was blown prematurely, resulting in the loss to the Japanese of two-thirds of the division's men, most of its transport, and all its artillery. This defeat, on February 22, decided the campaign.

Trouble with Australia again

After the fall of Singapore, it had been decided, with the agreement of the Dutch Government, that the 6th and 7th Australian Divisions, which had previously been allocated to the defence of Java and Sumatra, should return to their own country. As the convoy in which the two divisions was sailing was off Ceylon at the time of the attack on Burma, Churchill wished to divert one, if not both, of them to Rangoon. The only result was another rebuff from Mr. Curtin on February 23:

"4. With A.I.F. troops we sought to save Malaya and Singapore, falling back on Netherlands East Indies. All these northern defences are gone or going. Now you contemplate using the A.I.F. to save Burma. All this has been done, as in Greece, without adequate air support.

"5. We feel a primary obligation to save Australia not only for itself, but to preserve it as a base for the development of the war against Japan. In the circumstances it is quite impossible to reverse a decision which we made with the utmost care, and which we have affirmed and reaffirmed."

In this situation there can be no question but that the Australian Prime Minister was right. In so critical a situation, Churchill and the Combined Chiefs-of-Staff Committee would only have been writing off the division or divisions that ventured into this hopeless theatre of operations.

As it happened, the Burma area was on February 24 made a part of the India Command, under General Sir Harold Alexander, which in its turn had just come under Wavell's command. Alexander,

an optimistic and determined officer, took up command in Rangoon on March 5, and quickly realised that he was faced by problems very similar to those by which he had been faced at Dunkirk.

Rangoon abandoned

The capital of Burma was defended by the remnants of the 17th Indian Division, while the 1st Burma Division, made up of native battalions with British and Indian strengthening, was operating against the invaders to the north. But the defenders were so short of men that a 125-mile gap had opened up between the two divisions, and through this the Japanese were infiltrating in considerable numbers. Faced with this situation immediately after his arrival, Alexander had no alternative but to sacrifice part of the theatre under his command. His axe fell of the southern area: after its oil refineries

△ *Not British, but Americans (the British-style steel helmet was replaced by the distinctive G.I. "battle bowler" by the late summer of 1942). These are men from the surrendered fortress of Corregidor Island in Manila Bay, whose fall effectively ended the Philippine campaign.*

had been comprehensively destroyed, Rangoon was abandoned on March 7, the British retreating up the Irrawaddy valley to regroup their forces, now reinforced by the arrival of the British 7th Armoured Brigade, more infantry, and aerial reinforcements from Britain and China. Lieutenant-General William Slim was appointed to command these reorganised forces.

Alexander now decided that his primary strategic objective was the protection of the Yenangyaung oilfields, in which he was to be aided by the Chinese 5th and 6th Armies, under the command of Lieutenant-General "Vinegar Joe" Joseph Stilwell, the American officer who had been considered originally for the command of Operation "Super-Gymnast" but was now Chiang Kai-shek's military right hand. But co-operation with the Chinese proved difficult. A force equivalent in size to a British division was considered an army, and Chinese tactics bore very little resemblance either to Allied or Japanese ones. The following anecdote from Field-Marshal Lord Alexander's memoirs will serve to illustrate this:

"Before the battle of Mandalay I went round the front to inspect our defences and was much impressed to see how cleverly this Chinese Fifth Army had dug in its field guns, which were well sited and cleverly camouflaged. When contact had been gained with the advancing Japanese I again visited the front, and to my astonishment I found that the artillery had disappeared.

"When I asked the army commander what had happened to his guns he said that he had withdrawn them to safety.

" 'Then you mean,' I said, 'that they will take no part in the battle?'

" 'Exactly,' he replied.

" 'But then what use are they?'

"He said: 'General, the Fifth Chinese Army is our best army, because it is the only one which has any field guns, and I cannot afford to risk those guns. If I lose them the Fifth Army will no longer be our best.' "

Retreat to India

In the circumstances, upper Burma was no more defensible than lower Burma. The Japanese 15th Army had been reinforced by two more divisions and more

Corregidor: then and now

Corregidor was the "cork in the bottle" which the Japanese had to take if they wanted free access to Manila Bay. It was in fact the largest of a complex of island defences in the mouth of the bay of which the most impressive was Fort Drum, the "concrete battleship" El Fraile Island, shorn off, encased in massive concrete armour, and armed with 14-inch guns. Tadpole-shaped Corregidor is 3½ miles long, and only 600 yards wide at its narrowest point. The latter is also the lowest part of the island, and was known to the Corregidor garrison as "Bottomside". To the west was a plateau, "Middleside", and then the highest point of the island, "Topside". To the east, on Corregidor's "tail", is Malinta Hill, and under it Malinta Tunnel, connecting Bottomside with the eastern part of the island. Branching off the main tunnel were extensive laterals, with the garrison hospital on the north side. Troops were moved by electric railway (some 13½ miles of track in all), and there were also 65 miles of road. Corregidor's armament looked impressive on paper—56 coastal guns, with calibres ranging from 3-inch to 12-inch. There were also 72 A.A. guns—3-inch and .50-inch calibre. But Corregidor, like Singapore, had serious weaknesses, of which the most serious was the stock of ammunition. There were not enough heavy shells to neutralise the fire of the Japanese shore batteries which were set up when Bataan fell, and 3-inch A.A. ammunition was also low. The Japanese had time on their side and they used it well, silencing Corregidor's batteries and pounding away until all wire communications were dead. When they finally landed on the night of May 5–6, the 15,000-man garrison was so disjointed that no reserve could be found capable of repulsing little more than 1,000 Japanese. Wainwright finally surrendered at 1000 hours on the 6th.

△ ◁ Malinta Hill from the sea.
◁ Malinta Tunnel, running right across the island.
△▷ Ruined barracks at Topside.
▷ One of the 12-inch mortar batteries.

807

◁◁ *Japanese troops guard a mass of prisoners at the mouth of Malinta Tunnel on Corregidor.*
△ *Prelude to the notorious "Death March": American and Filipino prisoners are herded into column.*
◁ *A rest on the march.*
▽ *Journey's end for the survivors of the "Death March": approaching Camp O'Donnell, with those unable to walk being carried in improvised litters.*
▷ *How the war spread south and engulfed the "Southern Area".*

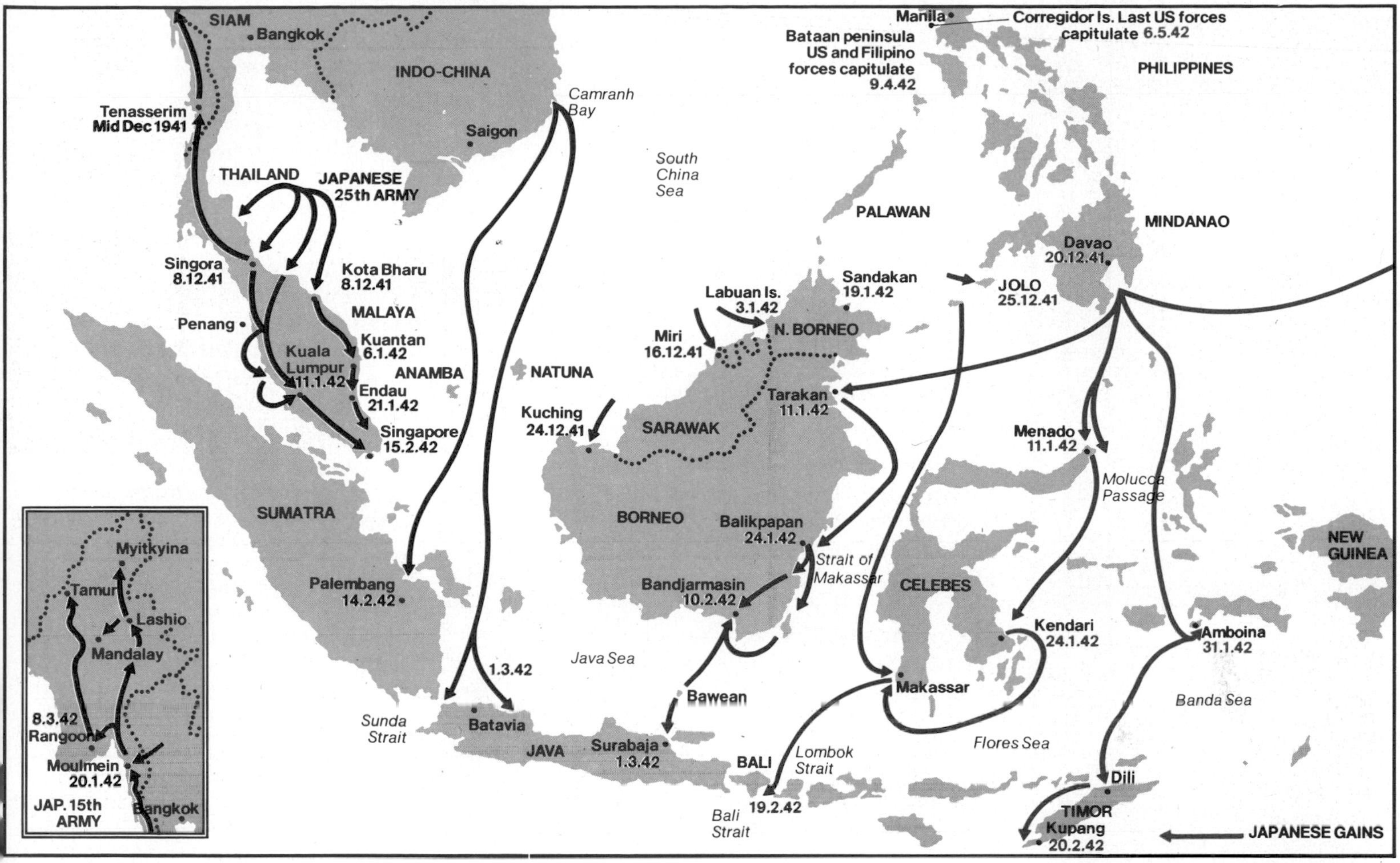

SIAM
Bangkok
INDO-CHINA
Tenasserim
Mid Dec 1941
Camranh Bay
Saigon
South China Sea
THAILAND
JAPANESE 25th ARMY
Singora 8.12.41
Kota Bharu 8.12.41
MALAYA
Penang
Kuala Lumpur 11.1.42
Kuantan 6.1.42
ANAMBA
Endau 21.1.42
Singapore 15.2.42
SUMATRA
Palembang 14.2.42
NATUNA
Kuching 24.12.41
SARAWAK
BORNEO
Miri 16.12.41
Labuan Is. 3.1.42
N. BORNEO
Sandakan 19.1.42
JOLO 25.12.41
Tarakan 11.1.42
Balikpapan 24.1.42
Strait of Makassar
Bandjarmasin 10.2.42
Java Sea
1.3.42
Sunda Strait
Batavia
JAVA
Surabaja 1.3.42
Bawean
BALI
Bali Strait
19.2.42
Lombok Strait
Makassar
CELEBES
Kendari 24.1.42
Flores Sea
Menado 11.1.42
Molucca Passage
Manila
Corregidor Is. Last US forces capitulate 6.5.42
Bataan peninsula US and Filipino forces capitulate 9.4.42
PHILIPPINES
PALAWAN
MINDANAO
Davao 20.12.41
NEW GUINEA
Amboina 31.1.42
Banda Sea
Dili
TIMOR
Kupang 20.2.42
JAPANESE GAINS
Myitkyina
Tamu
Lashio
Mandalay
8.3.42 Rangoon
Moulmein 20.1.42
JAP. 15th ARMY
Bangkok

aircraft just before the capture of Rangoon, and the British-Chinese line south of Mandalay had not the resources to hold the Japanese advance. In the middle of April the Japanese took Yenangyaung, though the Allies managed to sabotage the oil wells before they arrived. At the end of the month, on the 29th, the Japanese drove the Chinese 5th Army back over the border into China and occupied Lashio. Alexander, with his left flank exposed by the defeat of the Chinese, was forced to evacuate Mandalay, and retreat towards India across the Irrawaddy and Chindwin rivers. When the monsoon began, his little army was safe in the Indian state of Manipur after the longest, and one of the most gruelling, retreats ever carried out by the British Army.

The Japanese capped their victory in Burma by occupying the Andaman Islands, in which Port Blair offered them an excellent anchorage.

Nagumo's successes

The above advances by the Japanese land forces were matched by the successes of Vice-Admiral Chuichi Nagumo's Carrier Fleet. On January 20, planes from Nagumo's carriers bombed Rabaul on New Britain, and then this extremely important strategic point in the South-West Pacific was captured on the 23rd. Possession of this base gave the Japanese the choice of advancing either on New Guinea or the Solomons. On February 29, Japanese carrier-borne aircraft raided Port Darwin, on the north coast of Australia, sinking a dozen merchantmen in the harbour. A few days later, the Carrier Fleet was ordered to move south of Java, with the aim of preventing the evacuation of the island when the Japanese invaded from the north. Between March 3 and 5, repeated attacks were made on the port of Tjilatjap, causing the loss of three destroyers and 17 transports. On March 26, the Carrier Fleet sailed from Kendari, under the command of Vice-Admiral Kondo, to launch a surprise attack against targets on the island of Ceylon.

The Japanese fleet sent on this mission was a powerful one: five aircraft-carriers (with some 300 aircraft), four *Kongo*-class battleships (14-inch guns), two heavy cruisers, one light cruiser, and eight destroyers. As this force attacked Ceylon,

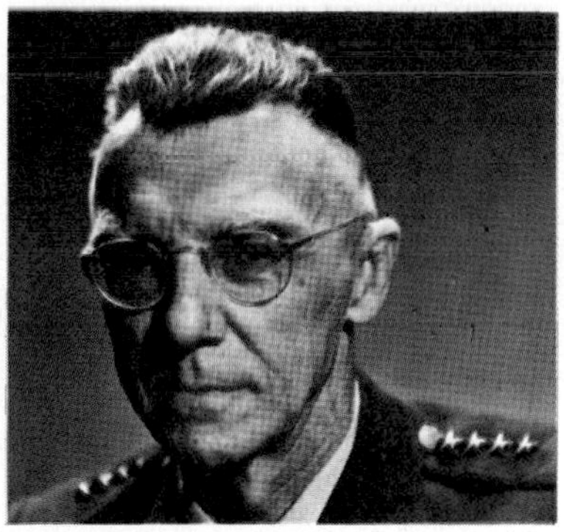

Lieutenant-General Joseph W. Stilwell was nominated by Roosevelt as chief-of-staff and general military adviser to Chiang Kai-shek, and arrived in Burma in February 1942. Thus his first experience of fighting the Japanese was the ultimate test of any general: fighting a retreat. He threw himself into the task of training the Chinese forces, and of instilling fighting spirit into Chiang and his generals. He had a thankless and frustrating job, way down on the list of Allied priorities.

△ *A Japanese tank in action in Burma. Japan's armour was frail and obsolescent—far inferior to contemporary German, Russian, American, or even British standards, but in a one-sided fight like the first Burma campaign this mattered little as opposition was minimal.*

▷ *Japanese troops occupy the oilfields at Yenangyaung in Burma—a key objective. However despite the pace of the Japanese advance the British had enough time to destroy the most important installations.*

another squadron, comprising the light aircraft-carrier *Ryujo*, six cruisers, and eight destroyers, was to carry out a raid in the Bay of Bengal, under the command of Vice-Admiral Ozawa. British reconnaissance aircraft had seen the beginning of this two-pronged attack, and the British War Cabinet became intensely worried lest the Japanese should try to obtain naval and air superiority in the Indian Ocean.

Britain's Eastern Fleet

The question had, in fact, been discussed by the Japanese. In order to take maximum advantage of their recent run of brilliant successes, this strategic aim appeared to be both possible and appropriate. Captain Kuroshima, head of the operations section of the Combined Fleet headquarters, supported the idea. In his opinion, it was advisable to make use of the respite gained by the neutralisation of the American forces in the Pacific to crush the British squadron in the Indian Ocean, conquer Ceylon, and advance on the Red Sea and Persian Gulf. The Japanese

forces would then advance to meet their Axis partners sweeping down from the Caucasus and east from Suez.

Realising that this possibility was on the way to becoming a probability after the fall of Malaya, Admiral of the Fleet Sir Dudley Pound made every effort to frustrate this dangerous scheme. To this end he assembled in the area of Ceylon the elements of a new fleet, under Admiral Sir James Somerville, the former commander of Force H at Gibraltar. On the day that Kondo and Ozawa sailed from Kendari, the Eastern Fleet, as the new British fleet was called, consisted of three aircraft-carriers (*Indomitable*, *Formidable*, and the aged *Hermes*), five battleships (*Warspite*, which had just returned from repairs in the U.S.A., and the four *Royal Sovereign*-class vessels, with a total of 40 15-inch guns), two heavy cruisers, five light cruisers (one of them Dutch), 16 destroyers, and seven submarines (two of them Dutch).

On his way out to take up his new command, Somerville wrote to Pound a masterly appreciation of the situation in the Indian Ocean: if the Japanese captured Ceylon "it will be extremely difficult, but not necessarily impossible, to main-

tain our communications to the Middle East. But if the Japanese capture Ceylon *and* destroy the greater part of the Eastern Fleet, then ... the situation becomes really desperate."

The British had learnt the lessons of the loss of *Prince of Wales* and *Repulse*, and now had a better appreciation than before of the relative strengths of the forces which might come into contact. Somerville realistically decided that it could not be in the Royal Navy's favour. Admittedly, the British fleet's 40 15-inch guns were superior to Kondo's 32 14-inch weapons, but to use this advantage, the four *Royal Sovereigns* would have to maintain contact with the *Kongos*, which were five knots faster. But more important was the question of defence. The British ships had been built in World War I and had been little modified, resulting in inadequate deck armour and A.A. armament. The Japanese naval aircraft, which were in every respect superior to their British counterparts, would have made short work of them.

Somerville had only about 100 out-of-date bombers and fighters to put up against more than 300 superior Japanese machines, which also had excellent crews. This disparity was clearly shown in an engagement off Colombo on April 5, when a formation of 12 Fairey Swordfish torpedo-bombers was surprised by Japanese Zeros and completely destroyed.

Luckily for the British, however, Captain Kuroshima's arguments were not accepted by his superiors. The Japanese push into the Indian Ocean was limited to attacks on Colombo and Trincomalee, which produced negligible results, thanks to Admiral Sir G. Layton's excellent counter-measures, which included the retention of three squadrons of Hawker Hurricanes intended for Java. These would have been lost or surrendered by March 9 had Layton let them go.

Hermes sunk

Colombo was bombed on April 5, though the raid missed the cruisers *Cornwall* and *Dorsetshire*, which had sailed late on the 4th. On the morning of the 5th, however, they were spotted by Japanese aircraft. An attack by 80 planes was swiftly mounted, and under a rain of bombs (about 90 per cent hit their targets) the two heavy cruisers sank. On April 9 *Hermes*,

which had been launched in 1919 and was one of the world's oldest aircraft-carriers, was caught by a raid as she was leaving Trincomalee harbour with the Australian destroyer *Vampire*. Both vessels were sunk. At the same time, Ozawa was attacking merchant shipping further to the north, where he sank 23 vessels, displacing a total of 112,312 tons. In the first ten days of the month, Japanese submarines operating in the area sank a further 32,404 tons. To the south again, the British were fortunate in evading Nagumo's aircraft, which were searching south-east of Ceylon, whereas the British fleet was in fact to the west of the island.

On April 7, however, the British Admiralty realised that the Japanese had not been deterred from advancing into the Indian Ocean by the Allied forces there, and authorised Somerville to withdraw to East Africa. Somerville decided to send his slower ships there while he himself, with the faster units, continued in the area. They would not use Sinhalese waters, though, but make their base at Addu Atoll (or "Port T") at the southern end of the Maldive Islands. But the defences of the island were so weak that Somerville, after assessing them, decided

△ *A Chinese soldier on the Burma front. Despite the hopeless vacillation and caution of their own commanders, there was nothing wrong with the fighting spirit of the Chinese rank and file. Stilwell's regard for the Chinese soldier was high. In a broadcast after the retreat from Burma he said: "To me the Chinese soldier best exemplifies the greatness of the Chinese people–their indomitable spirit, their uncomplaining loyalty, their honesty of purpose, their steadfast perseverance. He endures untold privations without a whimper, he follows wherever he is led without question or hesitation, and it never occurs to his simple and straightforward mind that he is doing anything heroic. He asks for little and always stands ready to give all."*

△▷ *For America the most enduring Japanese blow was naturally Pearl Harbor and the propaganda message was correspondingly simple: remembrance and revenge. But not even the Americans could resist the age-old propaganda line based on the fifth column and the "stab in the back".*

not to use the base and to stay at sea.

But soon the crisis passed. On April 12 the Japanese Combined Fleet had returned to Kure to prepare for its next offensive operations. Kondo and Ozawa returned to the Pacific, and major Japanese units never again entered the Indian Ocean.

Japan at high tide

This marked the end of the first phase of Japan's military expansion in World War II. General Tojo had occupied the "South-East Asia Co-Prosperity Sphere" which had been his major objective since coming to power. And he had obtained it at little cost: five destroyers, eight submarines, and 50,000 tons of merchant shipping at sea; and 10,000 dead and 4,000 wounded on land.

The Japanese advance into the Indian Ocean had presented the Allied command with the question of how to deal with the Vichy French colony of Madagascar, in particular the naval base at Diego-Suarez

in the far north of the island. As long as Churchill hoped to persuade Marshal Pétain and Admiral Darlan to support Operation "Gymnast", he turned a deaf ear to General de Gaulle's exhortations to him to occupy Madagascar. But Rommel's success in Cyrenaica postponed any landing in North Africa indefinitely.

Laval's return to power, on the other hand, raised Allied fears that Vichy might agree to hand over Madagascar, which controls the Moçambique Channel, to the Japanese. Churchill decided to wait no longer, and Operation "Ironclad" was launched on May 5, when naval and land forces under Rear-Admiral E. N. Syfret and Major-General R. C. Sturges captured Diego-Suarez. Further landings were made between September 10 and 29 resulting in the surrender of the final Vichy forces on November 6.

In fact the Japanese had no real interest in the Indian Ocean, and the invasion of Madagascar did nothing but prevent a threat that never existed and further exacerbate relations between Vichy and Great Britain.

CHAPTER 60
America and the U-Boat War

For the Allies, upon whom Roosevelt had conferred the somewhat grandiose title of "United Nations", 1942 had begun badly in South-East Asia, when the Japanese got within striking range of Australia. But still greater disaster was to strike them in the Atlantic, on the American east coast and in the Caribbean, extending well into 1943. This was, of course, the new U-boat offensive, which between January 1942 and March 1943 would account for 1,673 merchant ships, totalling about 8½ million tons.

On December 8, 1941, with the attack on Pearl Harbor by the Japanese, Hitler had lifted all the efficiency-limiting restrictions which he had imposed on the use of U-boats in the Atlantic. Three days later, the American *chargé d'affaires* was summoned to the Wilhelmstrasse and handed his passport. Dönitz was now free to fight the "tonnage war" in any way he pleased, with efficiency his only criterion, instead of being confined to those theatres where the tactical and technical countermeasures of the Royal Navy were becoming daily more effective.

At the end of 1941, Dönitz, as *Befehlshaber der Unterseeboote* or B.d.U. (Commander of Submarines), had 249 U-boats available, of which, however, 158 were undergoing trials or training in the Baltic; of the remaining 91 combat U-boats, various postings, at which Dönitz had protested vigorously but which had been ordered directly by the Führer, had deprived him of another 36 (of which 23 were caught in what Dönitz described as the "Mediterranean mousetrap"). Thus only 55 boats were left for duty in the vital Atlantic, a number still further reduced because some were under repair or being overhauled in their bases. Dönitz was left with only about a dozen units for active service in the Atlantic.

However, the crews of these units were magnificently trained, and the U-boats themselves were well-designed craft, tough, manoeuvrable, possessing a fair turn of speed and excellent endurance – at an average speed of 12 knots, Type IXC boats had a range of over 11,000 miles, sufficient to allow them to operate on the Atlantic coast of America for two or three

△ A spur for the shipbuilding industry. The Battle of the Atlantic amounted to a desperate race to build more ships than were being sunk.
▽ The fate of the straggler: a lone merchantman blazes furiously after being pounced on and bombed by the Luftwaffe while making for port.

weeks before returning to France. But all these qualities would have been useless had not the technical difficulties in the firing mechanism of their torpedoes, which had been a source of trouble, and even of danger, in 1940 and 1941, been finally remedied.

From December 9, 1941, therefore, Dönitz decided to unleash Operation "*Paukenschlag*" ("Kettledrum-roll") against American merchant shipping, to cash in on the latter's inexperience. But instead of the 12 Type IXC boats that he

had hoped to have in this operation, he could send out only five in the period between December 16 and 25, since Grand-Admiral Raeder, sticking very closely to the Führer's orders, refused to allow Dönitz to use any of the boats around Gibraltar, where six were on observation duty. The five boats actually sent out crossed the Atlantic undetected, and arrived on their stations on January 13. Two days later, four more Type IXC boats left Brest and Lorient to join them.

The U.S. totally unprepared

Between January and June, these German raiders, operating singly on the American eastern seaboard, achieved results that can only be compared with those of a pack of wolves let loose among a herd of sheep, although little more than a month had elapsed between Hitler's declaration of war on the United States on December 11 and the beginning of "*Paukenschlag*" in January. Many aspects of World War II remain controversial, but upon this, opinion is unanimous: America was totally unprepared to take part in a ruthless struggle of this nature.

Upon this subject the British and American official naval historians, Captain S. W. Roskill and Rear-Admiral S. E.

Morison, have expressed themselves with a discretion that does them credit, but which is nonetheless significant. On the other hand, Ladislas Farago, resuming his journalistic career after the war, expresses himself more frankly on the subject, on which he is, after all, an expert, having been head of a research department in U.S. naval Intelligence during the war. Similarly, Captain Donald Macintyre, one of the greatest British experts on anti-submarine warfare, has written quite uninhibitedly about this aspect of the war.

As far as the events at sea during the first half of 1942 are concerned, Farago's and Macintyre's comments fit in exactly with those made in the German camp, either in the memoirs of Dönitz or Wolf-gang Frank's *U-boats against the Allies*.

The defence of the American east coast, from Canada to Florida, was the responsibility of the American Atlantic Fleet, commanded by Admiral R. E. Ingersoll, who took over from Admiral King when the latter became Commander-in-Chief of the United States Fleet and set to work to remedy the effects of Pearl Harbor. Under Admiral Ingersoll's overall authority, the responsibility for the defence of this enormous coastline fell upon Vice-Admiral Adolphus Andrews who, according to Farago, never ceased calling attention to the woefully deficient resources available to him:

"For months before Pearl Harbor, while his country was flirting with war in the Atlantic, Andrews pleaded with Washington to send him the ships and men he needed desperately to protect his sea frontier. Again and again he was told they were needed elsewhere and none could be spared for him. Andrews, who saw clearly the shape of things to come, grew caustic in the face of Washington's do-nothing attitude. Once, upon his empty-handed return from a pleading mission to Washington in June, 1941, he spoke to Captain T. G. Stapler, his operations officer, bitterly about 'the futility of a national defense policy that always finds us weak instead of strong when war starts'."

Outmoded command structure

Little wonder, then, that when war was declared on America, Andrews had under his command only 12 surface vessels, three of which dated from World War I, and 103 aircraft, of which most were unfit for combat duty. Furthermore, whereas the British Admiralty was formally empowered to issue orders to R.A.F. Coastal Command, the same was not true in America, where, by a law dating from 1920, the U.S. Navy had authority only over aircraft of the U.S. Marine Corps and aircraft taken on board a ship, all other land-based aircraft coming under the orders of the Army. The consequences have been described by Captain Macintyre:

"U.S. Army pilots were neither trained in shipping protection duties nor to bomb small moving targets such as submarines. Nevertheless, at the outbreak of war it was upon aircraft of the U.S. Army that the U.S. Navy had to rely for anti-submarine patrols and searches. The inexperience and lack of training of the pilots no doubt made the shortage of aircraft of less consequence; but, in fact, in January 1942 the air effort in the area of the Eastern Sea Frontier, covering some 600 miles of the Atlantic coast, consisted of two daylight sweeps every 24 hours by six short-range Army bombers."

Even Churchill, in his memoirs, comments discreetly "...it is remarkable that no plans had been made for coastal convoys and for multiplying small craft."

△ *A German submariner negotiates a water-tight door between compartments. The cramped conditions inherent in submarine design meant that the men who sailed the boats had to develop considerable acrobatic skills.*

Churchill and Pound serious concern, King asserted that "a convoy with only an inadequate escort is worse than no convoy at all". The results of such a strategy made themselves felt with dramatic speed: proceeding individually along the coast and in the Caribbean, American tankers and cargo vessels were sunk individually, while Admiral Ingersoll's destroyers carried out utterly pointless daily offensive patrols.

Indeed, although on April 1 a communiqué from the Secretary of the Navy announced that 28 U-boats had been sunk by the Atlantic Fleet since January 1, post-war documents show that the first U-boat to be sunk in this particular sector was not claimed until January 14, when the American destroyer *Roper* accounted for *U-85*, commanded by Lieutenant Greger. By that date, other Allied escorts had eliminated no less than seven U-boats.

Anti-British bias

One of the reasons that Admiral King was slow to adapt to the new conditions created by the German operations, and benefit from the Royal Navy's great experience in this field since September 1939, was that he felt little esteem for Great Britain or her navy. The memoirs of Admiral Cunningham and Field-Marshal Alanbrooke may be viewed with some suspicion of natural counter-bias, but Farago's judgement, being from a fellow American, may be accepted:

"In his innermost mind, he harboured a dormant prejudice against anything British. It was aggravated by jealous resentment of Britain's long predominance (and occasional arrogance) as a seapower, and probably it also was a subconscious compensation for the humiliation King felt his Navy suffered when it was so badly bested by Dönitz just as the British appeared to be getting the upper hand. I believe these intangible sources of his anti-British sentiment played as great a part in his mind as such strictly professional considerations as his insistence upon a vigorous prosecution of the war in the Pacific for which, he thought the British had but tepid enthusiasm."

On the German side, Dönitz has described the first phase of his new Atlantic offensive in the following words:

"Our success was complete. Ships sailed

LIFE-LINE OF FREEDOM
★ THE ★
MERCHANT MARINE ★
★

Whose fault?

Such lack of preparation must be blamed, not only on the American military chiefs, but also upon members of the Washington administration, beginning with Navy Secretary Frank Knox and President Roosevelt himself, who by the terms of the constitution was the commander-in-chief of all the American armed forces. But it must be said that Admiral King himself was slow to grasp the extent and seriousness of the crisis, and to recommend the tried and tested British remedies necessary to overcome it. On March 19, at a time when American losses were causing as if it was still peace-time. There was no black-out on the coast, the cities remaining brightly lit; the only exceptions were the lighthouses and buoys, whose lights were slightly reduced. Ships were still normally lit. Although war had been declared nearly five weeks before, no serious anti-submarine measures appeared to have been taken. Destroyers did, of course, patrol the shipping lanes, but with such clockwork regularity that our boats got to know when they would be coming round, and in between these times would be perfectly safe. There were a few depth-charge attacks, but they were never kept up long enough, although the shallow water would have given a high success rate. Their aircraft crews were completely inexperienced.

"Merchant ships were completely free with the use of their radios, often indicating their positions, and so giving our raiders valuable information. It was glaringly obvious that ships' captains had no idea of the circumstances in which

possible. The result was that from mid-February Dönitz was able to include the Caribbean in his offensive, and to attack tankers leaving Venezuela, Trinidad, and Curaçao–U-boats even fired on the refineries on the two islands.

On April 22, 1942 the new U-boat *U-459*, commanded by Lieutenant-Commander von Wilamowitz-Mollendorf, supplied its fellow submarines 500 miles north-east of Bermuda, a new idea to extend the operational radius of the active boats. Soon other German submarines were fulfilling the same task. These large 1,688-ton Type XIV "milch cow" submarines possessed only anti-aircraft guns in the way of armament, but were able to carry 700 tons of oil fuel, sufficient to replenish the tanks of a dozen U-boats in the Caribbean, or four if they went down as far as the latitude of the Cape of Good Hope. Thus Dönitz was able to keep 27 boats at sea between Nova Scotia and British Guiana, while the "milch cows" doubled the endurance of the U-boats in their area.

◁ △ *Finishing off another victim on the surface.*
◁ ▽ *Poster for the American merchant navy. Unlike its British counterpart, the American mercantile marine had been totally unprepared for war and its initial losses were appallingly high. And they remained so until the Americans painfully learned the lessons which had been absorbed by the British since September 1939.*

they might be attacked, and never dreamed that night surface attacks might be made on them.

"Our U-boats soon found the best tactics: by day they would remain on the sea-bed at a depth of between 150 and 300 feet, a few miles off the shipping lanes; and then at dusk they would move in towards the coast, and when it was quite dark they would surface in the middle of the enemy shipping."

The large Type IXC boats which formed the initial attacking group were soon joined by some smaller Type VIIC craft which, thanks to the enthusiasm and technical skills of their crews, pushed themselves to the utmost and managed to attain ranges hitherto thought im-

Hitler's "Norwegian complex"

To sum up, during the first half of 1942, the only man capable of threatening the success of Operation *"Paukenschlag"* was Adolf Hitler who, for reasons best known to himself, had returned to his obsession of the previous autumn–that Norway was the "zone of destiny". On January 22 he declared that "we must send reinforcements there, both submarines and surface vessels, neglecting all other considerations if necessary." He thought better of it soon afterwards, but on February 6 he

△ *The dream of every anti-submarine patrol: a U-boat running on the surface.*

The German Focke-Wulf Fw 200C-2 Condor maritime reconnaissance bomber

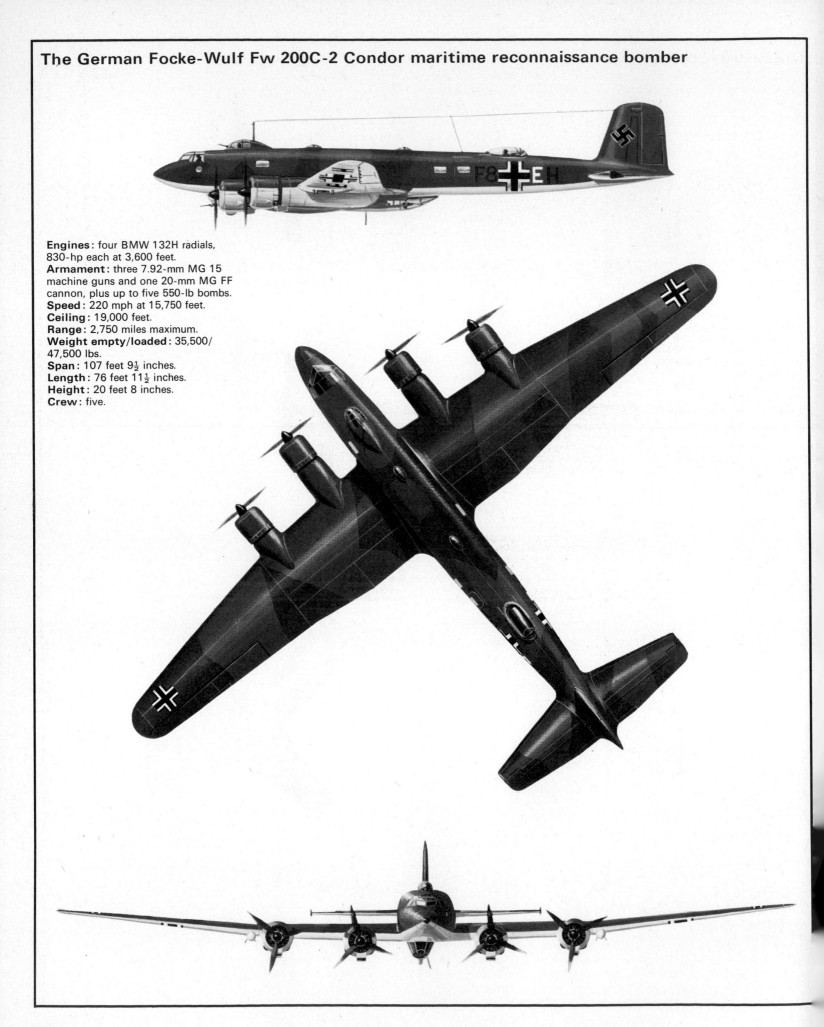

Engines: four BMW 132H radials, 830-hp each at 3,600 feet.
Armament: three 7.92-mm MG 15 machine guns and one 20-mm MG FF cannon, plus up to five 550-lb bombs.
Speed: 220 mph at 15,750 feet.
Ceiling: 19,000 feet.
Range: 2,750 miles maximum.
Weight empty/loaded: 35,500/ 47,500 lbs.
Span: 107 feet 9½ inches.
Length: 76 feet 11½ inches.
Height: 20 feet 8 inches.
Crew: five.

The British Short Sunderland Mark I flying boat

Engines: four Bristol Pegasus XXII radials, 1,010-hp each.
Armament: six .303-inch Browning machine guns and two .303-inch Vickers K machine guns, plus four 500-lb or eight 250-lb bombs.
Speed: 210 mph at 6,500 feet.
Ceiling: 17,000 feet.
Range: 2,900 miles maximum.
Weight empty/loaded: 27,190/50,100 lbs.
Span: 112 feet 8 inches.
Length: 85 feet 8 inches.
Height: 17 feet 9 inches.
Crew: up to ten.

ordered that eight U-boats be posted around the shores of Norway. Dönitz's reaction was to retort that the best way of defeating any possible attempt on Norway was to sink Allied shipping in the North Atlantic. His arguments, however, were not backed up by his superior, Grand-Admiral Raeder, and he had to submit to Hitler's wishes. Thus six U-boats, with their well-experienced crews, which Dönitz had been about to send off to the richly-promising American east coast, were sent off on patrol between Iceland and the Faeroes, on the look out for non-existent invasion forces.

Such was the effect of the Führer's "Norwegian complex", if it may be so called, on the strategy of the *Oberkommando der Kriegsmarine* (O.K.M.) or Navy High Command. And this was also a time when a single-minded application of the principle of concentrating one's energies on one object would have paid handsome dividends.

Captain Roskill's summing-up of this episode must command general agreement:

"Inevitably the weight of the offensive off the American coast declined, just at a time when it had proved highly profitable. In actual fact, the U-boats stationed between Iceland and the North Channel accomplished little in February and March, though two homeward convoys (S.C. 67 and H.X. 175) and two outward ones (O.N. 63 and O.N.S. 76) were attacked in those waters."

British and American losses

According to Admiral Dönitz, the untimely and quite useless depletion of his forces resulting from Hitler's decision about Norway meant that the German submarine forces sank half a million tons of shipping less than they would otherwise have done between January and June 1942. Even so, the U-boats were doing as well now as they had been at the height of the previous year.

But the figures opposite take no account of the losses incurred in the Mediterranean, Indian Ocean, or Pacific, in which theatres, according to Roskill, losses amounted to 287 ships of 625,000 tons. Furthermore, during the first quarter of 1942, 30 new U-boats entered service with the German Navy, whereas only 11 were sunk by the Allies. The situation was becoming hourly more desperate.

Churchill's alarm when faced by this situation was perfectly understandable. On February 10 he took the initiative in offering the U.S. Navy ten corvettes and 24 trawlers fitted with the latest asdic. On March 12 he decided to inform the President of British fears, which he did via Harry Hopkins. Presenting Hopkins with the grim statistics, he further added:

"The situation is so serious that drastic action of some kind is necessary, and we very much hope that you will be able to provide additional escort forces to organise immediate convoys in the West Indies-Bermuda area by withdrawing a few of your destroyer strength in the Pacific, until the ten corvettes we are handing over to you come into service."

To convince the President still further Churchill enclosed with his letter an eloquent map, graphically illustrating the absolute massacre of Allied shipping by U-boats in January–March 1942.

▽ *Loading up with torpedoes before another patrol–always a cumbersome, awkward business.*

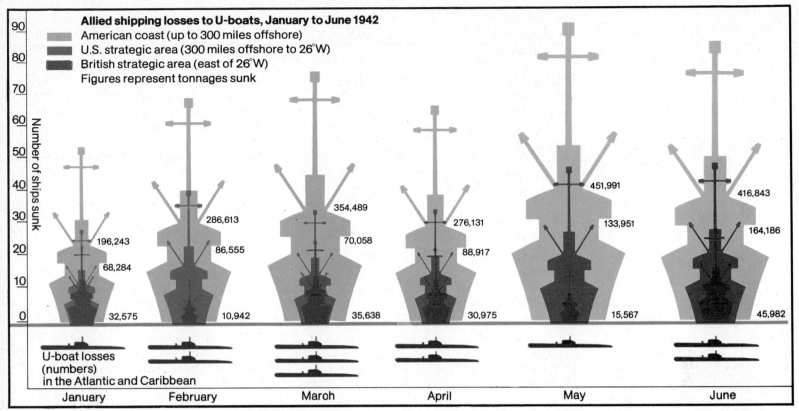

But Roosevelt, far from accepting Churchill's point of view, seems to have been rather piqued by the Prime Minister's action. On March 20 he replied somewhat curtly:

"Your interest in steps to be taken to combat the Atlantic submarine menace as indicated by your recent message to Mr. Hopkins on this subject impels me to request your particular consideration of heavy attacks on submarine bases and building and repair yards, thus checking submarine activities at their source and where submarines perforce congregate."

It is, however, only too easy to give advice: Churchill did indeed try to follow Roosevelt's urgings, but with the meagre resources available to it in 1942, the R.A.F. could not possibly succeed in the mission Roosevelt had so blithely suggested.

Divided energies

If Ladislas Farago is to be believed, the U-boat menace was not the problem which most concerned Roosevelt at this time. In fact it came some way down the list, after the air attack on Tokyo being prepared by General Doolittle, the enquiry into the disaster at Pearl Harbor, relations with Vichy, and, above all, keeping Russia in the war. But is Farago

right? It seems likely, as the U-boat problem is nowhere mentioned in the Hopkins papers referring to this period, and we know how close to the President Hopkins was. There was, therefore, a contradiction in the President's thinking: he wished the highest priority to be given to supplying military assistance to the Soviet Union, yet was more or less indifferent to the U-boat threat, which posed a permanent threat to this assistance. With every ship that was sunk in the Atlantic, a precious cargo of arms, ammunition, and other supplies was lost – equivalent to a defeat in battle.

In July 1942, convoy P.Q.17, bound for Archangel, lost 22 ships at the hands of the Luftwaffe and U-boats, with the consequent loss of 3,350 jeeps and trucks, 350 tanks, 210 aircraft, and nearly 100,000 tons of munitions, spare parts, food, armour plating, and other war supplies.

It is all too easy to regard such figures as a mere list of military hardware and spare parts. But as B. B. Schofield points out, the material lost with the victims of P.Q.17 was sufficient to have equipped an army – and in the middle of 1942, the most crucial year of the war, losses such as these could not be contemplated by the Allies.

Churchill had been aware of the importance of these losses since the very beginning of the crisis, but in Washington, it was not until June 19 that General Marshall pointed out to Admiral King

△ *The chart which marked Britain's chances of surviving, let alone of winning the war: tonnage losses versus U-boats sunk.*

△ *Sinking a merchantman with gunfire—far cheaper than using torpedoes and just as effective.*

of escort craft available, but has every conceivable improvised means been brought to bear on this situation? I am fearful that another month or two of this will so cripple our means of transport that we will be unable to bring sufficient men and planes to bear against the enemy in critical theatres to exercise a determining influence on the war."

America adopts the convoy system

On April 1, however, the U.S. Navy organised its first convoys along the east coast. But lacking adequate escorts the convoys had to anchor each night in protected harbours, after daily stages of less than 150 miles. Continuous convoys between Halifax, Nova Scotia, and Key West in Florida could not be instituted until the end of May.

that the whole of the U.S.A.'s war policy was being undermined by the ruthless German offensive.

"The losses by submarines off our Atlantic seaboard," he wrote in his historic memorandum to Admiral King, "and in the Caribbean *now threaten our entire war effort.* The following statistics bearing on the subject have been brought to my attention:

"Of the 74 ships allocated to the Army for July by the War Shipping Administration, 17 have already been sunk.

"Twenty-two per cent of the bauxite fleet has already been destroyed. Twenty per cent of the Puerto Rican fleet has been lost.

"Tanker sinkings have been 3.5 per cent per month of tonnage in use.

"We are all aware of the limited number

Faced with this new situation, Dönitz, though continuing with attacks by single U-boats in the Gulf of Mexico and in the Caribbean, where convoys could not be formed, recalled his U-boats operating off the east coast of the U.S. to the middle of the Atlantic, where they again began to hunt in packs, as before. He had great success in the second quarter of 1942, especially as the number of U-boats under his command was growing continuously and the trans-Atlantic convoys had been somewhat weakened by the organisation of the convoys from Halifax to Key West. Consequently, Allied losses in the spring of 1942 were even heavier than in the previous winter, this causing General Marshall to write to Admiral King the memorandum quoted above. No less than 455 ships, of more than two million tons total displacement, including a catastrophic proportion of tankers, were sunk—and this in the Atlantic and Caribbean alone, and excluding all but losses to U-boats.

In his answer to General Marshall, Admiral King now took up an attitude diametrically opposed to that which he had adopted in March, when he had cast grave doubts on the efficacy of the convoy system. On June 21 he wrote:

"Escort is not just one way of handling the submarine menace; it is the *only* way that gives any promise of success. The so-called patrol and hunting operations have time and again proved futile."

▽ *An ocean rendezvous for two of the "grey wolves".*

What was needed, therefore, was a large number of escort vessels capable of crossing the Atlantic, backed up by the new escort carriers. The alarm expressed by Marshall also gave King the chance to ask for a decision in his favour in the argument raging between himself and General Arnold about the allocation of anti-submarine aircraft. King estimated his needs as 1,350 aircraft, but the Army Air Force intended to supply him with only 500 medium-range bombers. Given these ships and aircraft, trans-Atlantic convoys could be covered during their whole crossing. Finally, King insisted that all operations in any way connected with the battle of the Atlantic should be centralised under his direct command.

Thus King, once he had realised his earlier mistakes, set to work to remedy the situation with a rational and well-balanced programme carried out energetically and clear-sightedly. Even so, nearly a year was to pass before his measures could begin to take effect, and much could happen in the interval. For example, none of the destroyer escorts ordered in the autumn of 1941 would come into service before the spring of 1943. But meanwhile the Allies would have to make do with the means at their disposal, and these were far from satisfactory as they stood.

In Paris, to which he had transferred his H.Q. after the St. Nazaire raid in March, Dönitz was also a worried man. To replace the 12 U-boats lost in the Atlantic in the first six months of the year, he had received 41 new craft, of which Hitler had taken 26 for the defence of Norway and two for the Mediterranean. The policy of dispersion of effort was still, therefore, being practised in Germany. But this was not all: while the U-boats in the Caribbean were having an easy time of it against the Americans, their fellows in the central and north Atlantic were running into greater and greater difficulties against British convoys whose escorts were growing ever stronger and more experienced.

On June 17, Dönitz radioed the following question to Lieutenant Mohr, commander of *U-105* and one of Germany's ablest U-boat captains, just as he was attacking a convoy sailing from Nova Scotia: "Have you personally noted the use by the enemy of surface detection apparatus?"

Mohr's negative reply was only partially reassuring, for U-boats sailing on the surface in the Bay of Biscay *had* been subjected to air attacks in circumstances admitting of no other explanation, despite the scepticism of German electronics experts. Dönitz notes in his memoirs:

"Aircraft came in from behind the sun,

△ *Help for a British destroyer, listing heavily after hitting a mine. Despite the fact that the initial danger of the magnetic mine had been averted, mines continued to exact heavy losses during the Battle of the Atlantic.*

△ △ A Focke-Wulf Condor runs up its engines before taking off at Bordeaux-Merignac for Atlantic patrol.

△ A Sunderland takes off. Until there were enough aircraft-carriers to go round, long-range flying boats offered the best means of providing cover for the convoys.

or suddenly emerged from behind a cloud, a fact which led us to believe that they had taken up position out of sight of the U-boat, whose position must therefore have been known. In June some of our vessels were bombed during the darkest nights. A searchlight would suddenly come on 1,500 to 2,000 yards away, illuminate the target immediately, and then the bombs would start to fall almost straight away. Three U-boats damaged in such attacks had to return to base."

The "wizard war"

Although he managed to obtain the use of 24 Junkers Ju 88's from the Luftwaffe to counter the activities of Coastal Command, on June 24 Dönitz was forced to order his boats not to surface while passing through the Bay of Biscay except to recharge their batteries. This had the unfortunate consequence for the Germans of greatly reducing their U-boats' operational radius.

Until they could be fitted with radar similar to that fitted to surface vessels, the U-boats were equipped with *"Metox"* apparatus, which recorded the British radar impulses and could thus tell the U-boats' captains when they had been spotted. But the *"Metox"* apparatus was designed to receive on the 150-cm wavelength, whereas the British and Americans were in the process of installing new equipment which operated on the 10-cm wavelength. This allowed the Allied anti-submarine patrols to spot the conning tower of a U-boat at a range of up to five miles. Thus, good as the German *"Metox"* was, it was obsolete by the standards of the improved British radar.

Dönitz was luckier with the *"Pillenwerfer"* (pill-thrower), which on several occasions enabled his U-boats to throw their pursuers off the scent. As soon as a U-boat commander heard the "ping" of Allied asdic on the hull of his boat, he would discharge a *"Bold"*, or cylinder filled with calcium carbide, which made the sea literally boil in its wake. For a quarter of an hour the boiling sea would send back false echoes, and give the U-boat a chance to escape. With time, however, the asdic (or sonar as it was called in America) operators became more skilful at distinguishing between *"Bold"* echoes and the real thing, and could no longer be tricked.

The tactic of hunting in packs presupposed a continuous exchange of information between U-boats at sea, and also between U-boats and their bases. But the British and Americans were able, however, to take advantage of this from the autumn of 1942 onwards by fitting their escort craft with H/F D/F (High Frequency Direction Finder or "Huff-Duff"), which enabled them to fix the position of a U-boat transmitting, up to a range of 25 miles away. Thus when a U-boat was discovered in the vicinity of a convoy, it was a simple matter to alter course away from the area, while sending in an escort to attack the U-boat. Meanwhile, the convoy, with the rest of the escort, would be steaming away from the place where the attack might be expected. Farago goes so far as to assert that these U-boat conversations, picked up by "Huff-Duff", precipitated the defeat of Germany's U-boat arm. This is a possibility, but it is difficult to see what else the U-boats

could have done to make their pack tactics work, especially as these tactics were the only ones to achieve success.

At all events, what Churchill called the "wizard war" was at its height, and on August 21, faced with the constantly increasing number of British and American aircraft now helping in convoy duties, Dönitz noted in his diary:

"The difficulties to be expected from that direction could lead to heavy, even disastrous, losses, to less successful results, and therefore to a lessening of the possibility of success in the submarine war."

For Coastal Command was increasing its strength, though less quickly than its commander, Air Chief-Marshal Sir Philip Joubert de la Ferté, would have liked, as Bomber Command had higher priority. Nevertheless, by mid-1942 Coastal Command did have 709 aircraft available, of which 16 were of the new Consolidated B-24 Liberator type. And at the same time the Americans and Canadians were increasing their anti-submarine air forces. Little by little, the "North Atlantic gap" was being plugged.

Brazil declares war on Germany

Following instructions from the German Foreign Ministry, U-boats operating in the South Atlantic now extended their attacks to Brazilian shipping, and on August 22 the Brazilian Government reacted to these acts of aggression with a formal declaration of war. Both Dönitz and Roskill maintain that the Germans committed a grave error—American aircraft could now be based at Pernambuco and Natal, in Brazil, thus tightening Allied control of the South Atlantic by co-operating with R.A.F. aircraft from Freetown, Bathurst, and Takoradi in West Africa.

Dönitz's renewed aggression

The turn for the worse that events had taken only served to increase Dönitz's attacks on Allied merchant shipping. Between July 1942 and May 1943 the

△ *More comments on the Battle of the Atlantic. This one, from Munich's* Simplicissimus, *reads: "Hurry, lads, the new Lend-Lease Law's come into force!"*
▽ *From the other side of the Atlantic* (Christian Science Monitor, *of New York)—a U-boat tells a fisherman's tale to Hitler: "And then I got one this big!"*

△ *American plea for more production and quicker deliveries of war material.*

balance swayed first one way, then the other, until Dönitz was forced on the latter date to admit defeat, for the time being at least. His forces had, in fact, fought magnificently, and his crews, their increased numbers notwithstanding, had performed miracles of skill and courage.

During this second half of 1942, the German U-boats turned their attentions away from the Caribbean and the American east coast to three sectors of the Atlantic: the area between the Newfoundland Bank and Iceland; off Freetown and Cape Green; and off the mouth of the River Orinoco and around Trinidad. In all these areas they exacted a heavy toll of Allied shipping. A few examples will suffice to show this:

Between August 5 and 10, convoy S.C.94, made up of 36 merchantmen and six escorts, lost 11 cargo vessels in the North Atlantic, though the Germans lost two U-boats;

On the same route, between October 10 and 15, convoy S.C.104, of 44 ships, was attacked by a pack of 13 U-boats and lost eight vessels, seven of them to *U-221* (Lieutenant Trojer); in reply, the escort of two British destroyers and four Norwegian corvettes sank two U-boats, *U-619* and *U-353;*

Worse was to follow: between October 26 and 30, convoy S.L.125, *en route* from Freetown to London, was attacked between the Canary and Madeira islands, and lost 13 of its 37 ships. The escort was unable to claim a single kill. However, as Captain Roskill has pointed out, the U-boats which converged on this convoy left the way open for the first transport vessels for Operation "Torch".

Finally, between October 1 and November 7, and at the cost of only one U-boat sunk off French Guiana by an American bomber, 25 tankers and cargo vessels were sunk by U-boats in the waters around Trinidad.

Taking into account the production capacity which his department credited to the British, American, and Canadian shipyards, Dönitz reckoned that for the battle of the Atlantic to be won decisively by the Germans, 700,000 tons of Allied shipping would have to be sunk each month. This figure was reached in June (700,235 tons), and improved upon slightly in November (729,160 tons). In December, however, because of the new theatre of operations opened up in North Africa by the "Torch" landings, and the consequent need to post a considerable number of

U-boats in the approaches to the Strait of Gibraltar, less than half the required tonnage was sunk (330,816). But the Atlantic was not the only area in which the tonnage war was being fought out nor was the U-boat the only weapon in the Axis arsenal.

The British fuel crisis

Overall, during 1942 the Western Allies lost a total of 1,664 ships (7,790,967 tons) of which 1,160 ships (6,266,155 tons) were sunk by German and Italian submarines. To this figure must be added a million tons of shipping unavailable as it was under repair. During the same period, only 7,000,000 tons of new shipping were built.

This explains why British imports in 1942 fell to less than 34 million tons, two thirds of the tonnage that had been imported in 1939; as imports of consumer goods had been severely controlled from the beginning of the war, it was clearly vital war commodities that were being seriously threatened at this time, Captain Roskill tells us, the state of Britain's fuel oil supplies were beginning to give grave grounds for fear:

"In mid-December there were only 300,000 tons of commercial bunker fuel in Britain, and consumption was running at about 130,000 tons a month. The Admiralty held another million tons which could be used in an emergency, but if the naval stocks were allowed to run

down the fleet might be immobilised. 'An ample reserve of fuel on this side of the Atlantic is the basis of all our activities,' reported the Admiralty; and when the Prime Minister was given the figures quoted above, he minuted on the paper 'This does not look at all good . . .' "

A new commander

In November, Admiral Sir Percy Noble, having served his term as Commander-in-Chief, Western Approaches, handed over to Admiral Sir Max Horton a first-class organisation. Horton, a seasoned submarine commander in World War I, devoted the priceless commodities of experience and enthusiasm to his task.

In the German camp, Dönitz was faced by a problem: he had lost 87 U-boats, two in accidents, 15 in the Mediterranean, and 70 in the Atlantic. Only 17 of this last category had succumbed to American vessels and aircraft. However, as the number of U-boats built greatly exceeded that of losses, at the end of the year Dönitz had 212 craft instead of the 91 with which he had started the year, and 20 new boats were being commissioned each month.

Closer scrutiny of these figures justifies a less optimistic assessment of German success in the event of a prolonged war. Recovering from Operation *"Paukenschlag"* quickly, the Allies had begun to counter-attack vigorously, with the result

that U-boat losses in the second half of the year were four times greater than in the first half: 14 between January and July, 56 between July and December. Etienne Romat has given a most graphic description of the scene in a sinking submarine:

"A dreadful drama unfolds inside the submarine: the water gushes in through a hole in the mess-room forward of the control room. The batteries are flooded; the salt water comes into contact with their sulphuric acid and gives off dense, stifling fumes of that terrible chlorine gas, which is sucked up into the engine room by the still-functioning diesel engines. The men's lungs are burnt out even before the order to abandon ship reaches them.

"Slowly the poisonous fumes reach the forward positions. Commander Hoeltring, who has been taken on board after his own submarine has been sunk, leaps up from his bunk and dashes to the control room, where one of his men, too seriously hurt to move, is dying. The chloride fumes arrive just as he does so. Knowing that he is finished, the young sailor begs his captain to finish him off quickly; Hoeltring obeys: taking out his pistol he first shoots the sailor then, half-suffocated, puts a bullet through his own brain.

"In the control room there is a wild rush towards the fresh air. Throwing discipline to the winds, ratings and officers fight madly with fists and spanners to get up the ladder to that little round opening framing the blue sky."

△ *Across the Atlantic, Admiral Sir Max Horton took over from Admiral Sir Percy Noble as Commander of the Western Approaches—a new foe for Dönitz. Energetic and supremely capable in himself, he also had the advantage of inheriting the splendid work of Noble.*

△△ *Convoy at sea. Station-keeping and smoke control was constantly dinned into the merchant captains.*

827

CHAPTER 61
The Channel Dash

◁ ◁ △ *Through the mist and gloom of February 12, 1942,* Scharnhorst, Gneisenau (*rear*) *and* Prinz Eugen *race through the English Channel, bound for German waters.*
◁ *Torpedo-boat flotillas gave a running escort to the capital ships as they headed up Channel.*

The contribution made by the German Navy's surface warships to the battle of the Atlantic was smaller than it had been previously, either because the loss of *Bismarck* had made Raeder more cautious about the use of his surface vessels, or— more probably—because the possibility of an Anglo-American landing in Norway had led Hitler to refuse to sanction the posting of any major vessels away from Germany. The contribution of the disguised raiders was also modest: from March to November, only 30 ships of 194,265 tons were sunk.

On January 14, *Thor* slipped out of the Gironde estuary. By the end of February she was in the Antarctic on the lookout for more whaling factory ships like those *Pinguin* had so profitably captured the year before. Drawing a blank there, however, *Thor* returned to the South Atlantic, where she made a few captures. During the summer, she moved into the Indian Ocean and after creaming off the ships plying between Ceylon and Australia, she passed through the Sunda Strait, preceded by her prizes, and docked in Yokohama on October 9.

Michel sailed from Germany on March 20 and managed to slip through the English Channel as the northern escape routes appeared impossible. For nine

▽ *Admiral Ciliax* (speaking at right), *who commanded the Brest Squadron of the German Fleet and led it through the Channel.*

months, thanks to the system of supply ships organised by the navy, she prowled the waters of the South Atlantic and Indian Ocean. Although she only just missed the big French liner *Pasteur*, which had been requisitioned by the British as a troopship, she did capture or sink 14 other Allied vessels of 94,362 tons. She arrived in Yokohama on January 1, 1943.

The third and last raider to reach the open sea was *Stier*, which sailed from Stettin on May 20, 1942. She reached the South Atlantic without difficulty via the English Channel and Bay of Biscay. Between July and September she sank two cargo ships and two American tankers. But on September 27 her fifth victim, the American ship *Stephen Hopkins*, proved her undoing. Although she had only one 4-inch gun against *Stier*'s six 5.9-inch weapons and two torpedo tubes, *Stephen Hopkins*, under the command of Lieutenant Kenneth Willett, took on *Stier* and managed to sink her, though she herself was also sunk. The crew of *Stier* were picked up by the German supply ship *Tannenfels*, but that of *Stephen Hopkins*

had to face four weeks in their life-boat before reaching Brazil. There were only 14 survivors from the American vessel.

On October 14 *Komet*, which was trying to join *Michel* and *Stier* in the South Atlantic, was intercepted and sunk by a force of five destroyers off Cape de la Hague in the Channel.

Surface forces redeployed

While Hitler's fantasy about an imaginary Allied threat to Norway greatly damaged Dönitz's U-boat offensive, it must at the same time be recognised that it led to a redeployment of the German Navy's surface forces which created considerable alarm in Great Britain and the United States, as their new positions constituted a powerful threat to the Allies' Arctic convoy route.

On the night of January 14, the battleship *Tirpitz*, which had completed her training in the Baltic, left Wilhelmshaven for Norway. On the 16th she reached Aasfjord, some 20 miles south of Trond-

△ *Before the British woke up to the fact that the big ships were out,* Scharnhorst, Gneisenau, *and* Prinz Eugen *had won a 300-miles start and were almost into the Dover Strait. E-boats, destroyers, and torpedo-boats formed the surface escort – but most important of all was the massive, multi-level air umbrella under the command of fighter pundit Adolf Galland.*

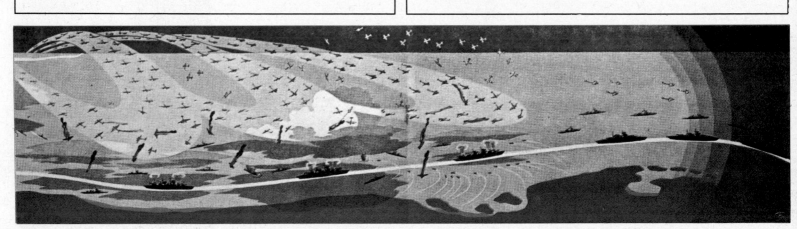

For German propagandists the Channel Dash came as a godsend. It was, after all, the most impressive performance put up by their surface ships since the *Bismarck* sank the *Hood*, and they made the most of it. This is how the episode was presented by the magazine *Signal*. It is a slick piece of work, but naturally fails to include every episode of the break-out. The original caption to the first-phase picture above, however, correctly makes the point that it took the British some 12 hours to wake up to the fact that the Brest squadron was coming up Channel, and by then *Scharnhorst*, *Gneisenau*, and *Prinz Eugen* were heading into the Straits of Dover at 30 knots.

With the second-phase picture the *Signal* illustration really goes in for some bending of the facts, showing a furious gunnery duel across the Channel between the British and German coastal batteries. "In the meantime the long-range guns at Dover opened fire. But the Luftwaffe's reply came at once. One after the other waves of aircraft bombed the British batteries. The German coastal guns fired salvo after salvo. The British fire, never accurate, began to fall short and diminished in intensity . . ." In fact the Dover guns only fired six salvoes and the German batteries only fired four—none of which did any damage. As for the Luftwaffe bombings of the Dover guns, they never happened at all.

The most tragic episode of the Channel Dash is not represented at all. It was Esmonde's Swordfish attack and it was beaten off with ease, all six Swordfish being shot down. Chaos reigned on the British side. Squadron-Leader Brian Kingcombe, leading the Spitfires which tried to shield Esmonde's Swordfish, recalls: "While making for a Messerschmitt I suddenly saw a beautiful bloody battleship and I thought to myself 'I never knew the Navy had such a lovely boat'. I was sure she was one of ours because she was heading straight for Dover. Anyway, no one had told me anything about German battleships being in the Straits." For the British this was the theme of the day.

The final phase in the *Signal* illustration show the German warships steaming serenely home to Germany. There is no mention at all of the crucial moments when *Scharnhorst* and *Gneisenau* both struck mines. Ciliax was later criticised for shifting his flag from *Scharnhorst*, which jeopardised the chain of command holding the squadron together. As it happened, *Gneisenau* and *Prinz Eugen* were "first home", and for some hours there was no knowledge of *Scharnhorst's* precise position. For all the rest of the squadron knew, she had been picked off after hitting her second mine. But she eventually struggled into Wilhelmshaven, steering gingerly into harbour by using her engines, as there were no tugs.

heim, where her crew immediately camouflaged her and laid anti-torpedo booms and nets. The appearance of *Bismarck*'s sister ship in Norwegian waters caused no little panic at the Admiralty, as Sir John Tovey, commanding the Home Fleet at Scapa Flow, had only *King George V* with which to engage *Tirpitz*, *Rodney* being too slow, *Renown* too unprotected, and *Duke of York* untrained. When he heard the news, Churchill breathed fire and slaughter. "The whole strategy of the war," he wrote to the chiefs-of-staff on January 25, "turns at this period on this ship, which is holding four times the number of British capital ships paralysed, to say nothing of the two new American battleships retained in the Atlantic. I regard the matter as of the highest urgency and importance. I shall mention it in Cabinet tomorrow, and it must be considered in detail . . .''

He therefore demanded the immediate planning of an attack on *Tirpitz* by the R.A.F. A torpedo attack was out of the question because *Tirpitz* was anchored in a part of the fjord where the attackers would not be able to make their run-in, so the attack was carried out by nine Handley Page Halifax and seven Short Stirling four-engined bombers of Bomber Command on the night of January 29. Not a single bomb hit its target.

The "Channel dash"

In November 1941, Raeder had been summoned to Supreme Headquarters in Berlin. Here he had proposed to Hitler that the heavy cruiser *Prinz Eugen*, which had lain idle in Brest since June, might return to Germany via the English Channel. "Why not the other two?" had been the Führer's immediate reaction, referring to the battle-cruisers *Scharnhorst* and *Gneisenau*, which were sharing *Prinz Eugen*'s enforced idleness. Hitler had not pressed the point at the time as Raeder objected to the idea strongly. But the question was raised again at the beginning of 1942, as Hitler wished to build up around Trondheim a force capable of countering any Allied attack on Norway.

On January 12, at a conference at Rastenburg, Raeder was forced to admit that an escape to Germany via Iceland was out of the question, the three crews no longer being at peak efficiency. And any attempt to break out up the Channel seemed to him to be pushing audacity to the point of folly. Vice-Admiral Ciliax, Lütjens's successor as *Flottenchef*, was less pessimistic; he thought that it could be done provided that absolute secrecy could be maintained and that the Luftwaffe could lend powerful air support from dawn to dusk on the day chosen for the operation. Colonel-General Hans Jeschonnek, Göring's chief-of-staff, and Adolf Galland, the General of Fighters, were both able to give their assurance for the second condition, and Hitler decided in favour of the operation.

"To come through the Channel is risky, but to stay in Brest is even more so," he said. "In any case the element of risk can be reduced if we take the enemy by surprise, which we can do if we send the ships through in broad daylight.

"The British are not capable of lightning decisions; and in any case, let us try to put ourselves in their place: what would we do if we were informed that an English squadron was sailing up north via the Pas-de-Calais? Could we, in the space of just a few hours, get together the aircraft necessary for a concerted attack? With our ships blockaded in Brest, we are in the position of a man ill with cancer; the operation is dangerous, but it is the only chance of survival, and therefore must be tried."

Bringing the meeting to a close, he declaimed: "You will see; Operation 'Cerberus' will be the greatest naval exploit of the whole war."

Admiral Ciliax's first condition—secrecy—could not be fulfilled, since in Brest Lieutenant Philippon was taking time off from his duties as officer in charge of the Navy's vegetable gardens to pass on information to London about the activities of

New menace in the north: Tirpitz, *sister-ship to* Bismarck, *holed up in a Norwegian fjord. When she moved north she upset the entire strategy of the Home Fleet, which was forced to keep sufficient capital ships at Scapa Flow to counter a possible break-out.*

the German warships there, and about their probable plans. On February 7, he sent this message: "Sailing imminent. Keep close watch at period of the new moon."

How they ran the channel

0028: German squadron passes Ushant, having left Brest shortly after midnight, February 11.
0114: Squadron swings east into Channel.
0530: Squadron passes Alderney.
0850: Low level fighter escort joins

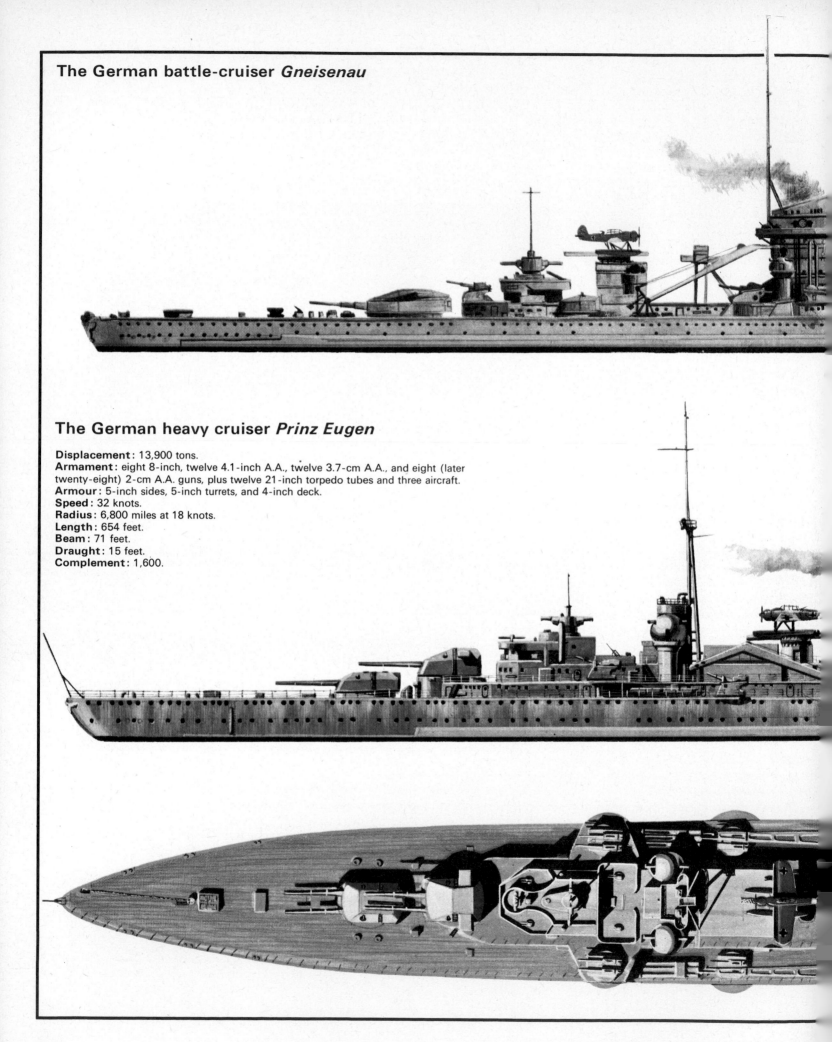

The German battle-cruiser *Gneisenau*

The German heavy cruiser *Prinz Eugen*

Displacement: 13,900 tons.
Armament: eight 8-inch, twelve 4.1-inch A.A., twelve 3.7-cm A.A., and eight (later twenty-eight) 2-cm A.A. guns, plus twelve 21-inch torpedo tubes and three aircraft.
Armour: 5-inch sides, 5-inch turrets, and 4-inch deck.
Speed: 32 knots.
Radius: 6,800 miles at 18 knots.
Length: 654 feet.
Beam: 71 feet.
Draught: 15 feet.
Complement: 1,600.

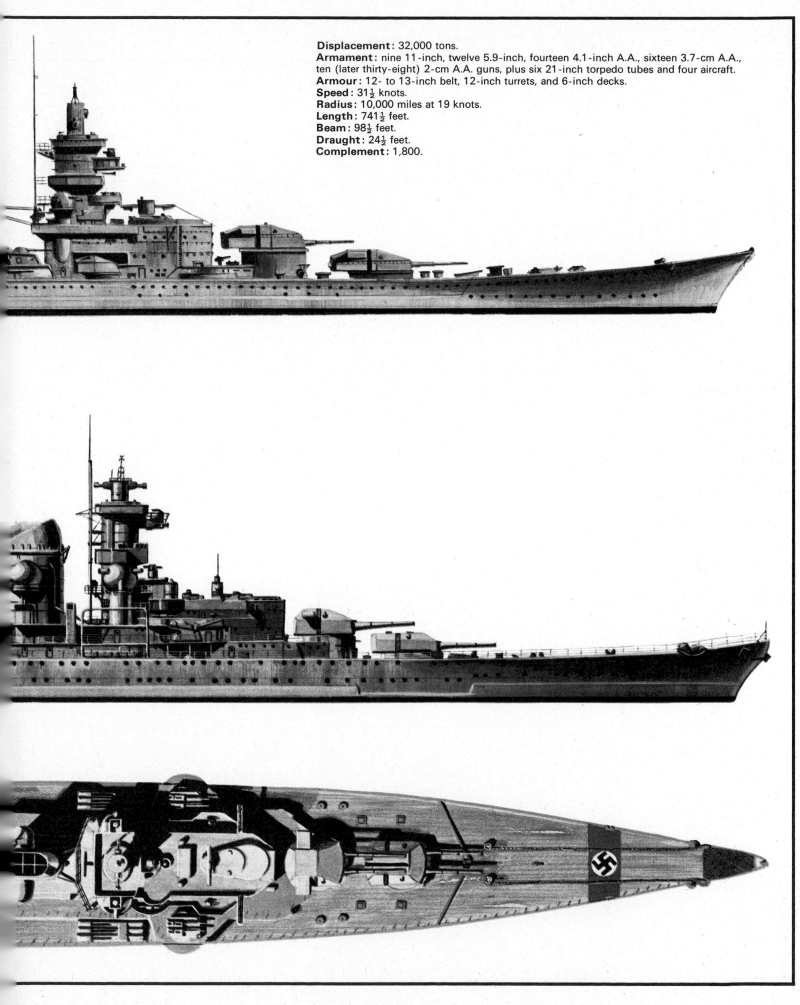

Displacement: 32,000 tons.
Armament: nine 11-inch, twelve 5.9-inch, fourteen 4.1-inch A.A., sixteen 3.7-cm A.A., ten (later thirty-eight) 2-cm A.A. guns, plus six 21-inch torpedo tubes and four aircraft.
Armour: 12- to 13-inch belt, 12-inch turrets, and 6-inch decks.
Speed: 31½ knots.
Radius: 10,000 miles at 19 knots.
Length: 741½ feet.
Beam: 98½ feet.
Draught: 24½ feet.
Complement: 1,800.

squadron north of Le Havre.

1042: Squadron sighted by Spitfire.

1219: Dover guns open fire.

1245: Esmonde's Swordfish attack is repulsed.

1430: *Scharnhorst* hits mine. Ciliax transfers to a destroyer.

1505: *Scharnhorst* under way again.

1547: British destroyers from Harwich attack unsuccessfully.

c. 1830: Last British air attacks on squadron, off Dutch coast.

1955: *Gneisenau* hits mine.

2134: *Scharnhorst* hits second mine.

Dawn, February 13: *Gneisenau* and *Prinz Eugen* arrive at Brunsbüttel.

0930: Ciliax returns to *Scharnhorst*.

1030: *Scharnhorst* arrives at Wilhelmshaven.

The fact that Operation "*Cerberus*" was successful is not due, as some have stated, to any scepticism at the Admiralty about this message, for Lieutenant Philippon was known as an absolutely reliable source of information; rather was it because the Admiralty interception plan assumed that the Germans would approach the Pas-de-Calais at night, and at high tide, which presupposed that they would leave Brest the previous afternoon. In fact, Admiral Ciliax left on February 11 at 2215; it so happened that the Coastal Command aircraft on patrol outside Brest harbour had a radar breakdown at that vital moment, and by a strange coincidence, a similar mishap befell the aircraft which was patrolling the Ushant-Brehat sector.

At 07 30 on February 12, the German warships caught their first glimpse of Galland's supporting fighters. It was not until three hours later, as they were passing Le Touquet, that they were at last identified by a British Spitfire. At 12 56 they entered the North Sea in line ahead and escorted by four destroyers, ten torpedo boats, numerous small craft, and covered by a very powerful air umbrella.

Suicide attack by Esmonde's Swordfish

When the Spitfire's report made what was happening crystal-clear, the British were totally unprepared, and their reaction was piecemeal, not to say quite unco-ordinated. In spite of the ten protecting fighters, the six Swordfish aircraft of Lieutenant-Commander Esmonde, who had previously distinguished himself in the encounter with *Bismarck*, were all shot down almost before they had time to launch their torpedoes. Their attack had bordered on the suicidal. A little later two flotillas of destroyers were thrown into the attack, but never got within striking distance. As for the R.A.F., 71 of the 398 aircraft which took part were lost, without a single bomb reaching its target, mainly because the Pas-de-Calais had an immense concentration of anti-aircraft guns, and the weather was deplorable.

Mines, however, were more successful; at 1431 *Scharnhorst* hit her first mine off the Scheldt estuary, and a second one in the evening as she passed Terschelling. With a thousand tons of water in her hull, and almost out of control, she nevertheless reached Wilhelmshaven, thanks to the coolness and excellent seamanship of Commander Hoffmann. Later that same evening *Gneisenau* struck a mine, but nevertheless managed to reach the Heligoland Bight.

British public opinion was furious at the success of Operation "Cerberus", and the War Cabinet was violently attacked in the press—*The Times*, for example, going as

▽ *A trophy for the Kriegsmarine's light units: this tattered White Ensign was taken after a clash between flotilla craft.*

far as to say that "Vice-Admiral Ciliax has succeeded where the Duke of Medina Sidonia [commander of the Spanish Armada] failed . . . Nothing more mortifying to the pride of sea-power has happened in home waters since the 17th Century."

The Times did not seem to realise that the German Navy's brilliant exploit–the result, be it remembered, of one of Hitler's happier inspirations–masked a strategic retreat, the abandonment of any further attempt to throw its capital ships into the tonnage war.

Nor was this all; *Scharnhorst* only managed to get back into Norwegian waters in March 1943, whilst *Gneisenau*, which was being repaired at Kiel, was so badly damaged by an R.A.F. bombing raid on February 26 that she was put into moth-

balls. *Prinz Eugen* came out of all this unscathed, and received orders, together with the pocket battleship *Admiral Scheer*, to get back to Trondheim, but was torpedoed *en route* by the submarine *Trident* (Commander G. M. Sladen), and had to turn back.

On March 21 the heavy cruiser *Admiral Hipper* reached "the zone of destiny", and on May 26, the pocket battleships *Lützow* and *Admiral Scheer* dropped anchor at Narvik.

Thus Hitler had recreated in Scandinavian waters a naval force of reasonable size, but quite unable to pass north of a line Scapa Flow–Iceland, since it would, in that event, have to face up to the Home Fleet, and behind that, the American Atlantic Fleet.

△ *The German squadron packed in a formidable concentration of A.A. fire power, and the flak gunners on the ships had a field day.*

1941

January

10. Lend-Lease Bill introduced to Congress.

13. Greece declines offer of British troops.

19. British advance in Eritrea, occupy Kassala in Sudan.

20. Roosevelt's third inauguration.

22. Tobruk falls to the British and Australians; 25,000 prisoners and 50 tanks taken.

29. Death of General Metaxas.

February

3. German battle-cruisers *Scharnhorst* and *Gneisenau* break out through the Skagerrak to the North Sea.

5. British armour engages Italians; fierce fighting near Benghazi.

6. British and Australians enter Benghazi.

8. Lend-Lease Bill passed by 260 to 165 in U.S. House of Representatives. First German troops leave Naples for North Africa.

10. Mussolini accepts Hitler's offer of a German armoured division. Cunningham's forces begin the advance into Italian East Africa.

12. Rommel arrives in Tripoli.

14. German units land in Tripoli. Yugoslav ministers meet Hitler.

22. Mr. Eden and Sir John Dill arrive in Athens. Rommel attacks at El Agheila.

23. Koryzis formally accepts the British offer of aid to Greece.

March

2. Eden and Dill in Athens. German troops enter Bulgaria.

4. British Commando raid on the Lofoten Islands.

6. Luftwaffe blocks the Suez Canal for three weeks with magnetic and acoustic mines.

7. Australian, British, and New Zealand troops land at Piraeus and Vólos.

8. U.S. Senate passes Lend-Lease Bill by 60–31.

12. Roosevelt requests Lend-Lease appropriation of $7,000,000.

19. Germany gives ultimatum to Yugoslavia.

23. British occupy Neghelli. R.A.F. raids Berlin.

24. Germans capture El Agheila. British force Marda Pass. British Somaliland clear of Italians.

25. Yugoslavia signs Tripartite Pact.

27. Revolution in Yugoslavia. King Peter takes over, forms new cabinet.

28. Battle of Cape Matapan.

30. German, Italian, Danish ships in U.S. ports seized. Rommel launches offensive in Cyrenaica. *York* sunk. R.A.F. attacks *Scharnhorst* and *Gneisenau* in Brest.

31. Eden and Dill in Athens.

April

3. Rashid Ali seizes power in Iraq. Benghazi abandoned.

5. Capture of Addis Ababa.

6. Germans invade Greece and Yugoslavia.

7. Generals O'Connor and Neame captured. Luftwaffe bombs Belgrade.

8. Massawa taken by the British.

9. Rommel takes Bardia. German armour reaches Salonika.

10. 9th Australian Division withdraws to Tobruk. U.S. moves into Greenland. Germans capture Zagreb.

11. Blitz on Coventry. Italian and Hungarian troops enter Yugoslavia.

12. Belgrade surrendered to the Germans. Allies form front on Mount Olympus.

13. Rommel encircles Tobruk. Stalin signs neutrality pact with Japan.

14. Germans repulsed at Tobruk. Germans force Klisura Pass.

18. Yugoslav Army capitulates.

22. Greek Army capitulates in Salonika. British begin to withdraw.

24. Germans break through at Thermopylai.

25. Germans capture Halfaya Pass; invade Lemnos; British pushed back to Marsa Matrûh. Führer Directive 28 orders attack on Crete.

26. German paratroops capture Corinth canal and town.

27. German troops enter Athens.

30. British evacuate last forces from Greece. Iraqi troops surround R.A.F. base at Habbānīyah.

May

2. Iraq demands withdrawal of British forces; British occupy Basra.

3. R.A.F. bombs Iraqi forces and aerodromes; Iraqis occupy Rutba and oil installations.

5. Haile Selassie returns to Addis Ababa.

6. British and native levies defeat Iraqi troops around Habbānīyah.

10. British force begins march to Baghdad. Hess flies to Scotland. House of Commons and British Museum hit in Luftwaffe raid.

12. "Tiger" convoy docks at Alexandria, lands 238 tanks. Luftwaffe raids Crete.

15. British retake Sollum and Halfaya Pass.

16. Last British reinforcements arrive in Crete. Duke of Aosta surrenders at Amba Alagi.

18. Italy annexes Dalmatia. Bulgaria occupies Macedonia. *Bismarck* and *Prinz Eugen* sail from Baltic.

20. German paratroops land in Crete in first stages of operation "*Merkur*".

21. Airborne invasion of Crete begins. Germans capture Máleme airfield. Royal Navy attacks German seaborne forces.

22. Freyberg orders withdrawal to shorter line. The Luftwaffe sinks cruisers *Gloucester* and *Fiji* and damages battleships *Warspite* and *Valiant* in heavy attacks near Crete.

24. *Hood* and *Prince of Wales* engage *Bismarck* and *Prinz Eugen*. *Hood* sunk.
25. Heavy fighting in Crete. *Bismarck* evades pursuers.
26. *Bismarck* located and disabled by aircraft torpedo. Freyberg orders withdrawal to Sphakia.
27. *Bismarck* sunk. Germans take Canea. Decision to evacuate Crete.
28. British evacuate Heraklion.
30. Iraq revolt collapses.

June

1. British enter Baghdad.
2. Hitler and Mussolini meet at the Brenner Pass. Vichy introduces laws on the status of Jews.
8. British, Australian, Indian, and Free French forces invade Syria.
15. Operation "Battleaxe" begins, mission to relieve Tobruk.
21. Damascus occupied by Free French forces. Auchinleck replaces Wavell as C.-in-C. Middle East.
22. Operation "Barbarossa" begins: Germany invades Russia.
23. Hungary and Slovakia declare war on the U.S.S.R. The Germans cross the river Bug.
24. Germans take Vilnius, Kaunas.
25. Finland attacked by Soviet Air Force.
26. Finland declares war on U.S.S.R. Germans capture Daugav'pils, river Dvina crossings, and Brest-Litovsk after four-day siege.
29. Göring nominated as Hitler's successor. Stalin, Malenkov, Voroshilov, and Beria form Defence Committee.
30. Vichy breaks off relations with the U.S.S.R.

July

. Germans capture Riga. Guderian's tanks cross the Berezina.
. Stalin calls for a "scorched earth" policy.

4. Tito announces resistance.
7. Vichy authorises the formation of a legion against Bolshevism.
8. Germany and Italy partition Yugoslavia.
9. Germans take Minsk pocket and Vitebsk.
11. Cease-fire in Syria. Voroshilov, Timoshenko and Budenny appointed commanders of North, Central, and South Fronts of the U.S.S.R.
15. Smolensk captured by Army Group "Centre".
20. Bock orders Guderian to close the Smolensk ring. Stalin has himself appointed People's Commissar for Defence.
22. German attack stopped at Lake Ilmen because of exhaustion.
24. Vichy agrees to Japanese occupation of Indo-China bases.
28. Japanese troops land in Indo-China. Japan freezes British, U.S., and Dutch assets.
31. U.S. recognises the Czechoslovak Government.

August

1. U.S. oil embargo on "aggressors".
3. Kleist, Stülpnagel seal Uman pocket. Mannerheim continues attacks to recover Karelian Isthmus, independently of German plans.
5. Rumanian troops begin 73-day siege of Odessa. Soviet resistance in Smolensk pocket ends.
7. Stalin becomes Supreme Commander.
12. Atlantic Charter signed by Churchill and Roosevelt. Army Group "North" advances on Leningrad.
19. British and Polish troops begin relief of Australians and Indians in Tobruk.
24. Russians counter-attack at Gomel; inflict heavy losses on the Rumanians at Odessa. Finns surround Russians at Vyborg.
25. British and Russian troops enter Persia. Commando raid on Spitsbergen.
26. British take Abadan.
27. British in Shahabad; Persian Government resigns.
Assassination attempt on Laval.
28. Cease-fire in Persia; Ali Furughi forms government.
29. Russians evacuate Karelian Isthmus.

September

1. Timoshenko counter-attacks in Gomel sector.
3. First use of gas chamber in Auschwitz.
5. Germans complete the occupation of Estonia.
8. Leningrad cut off by German tanks.
9. Persian Government accepts Anglo-Soviet terms.
11. Roosevelt gives the "shoot on sight" order to the U.S. Navy.
12. First snow on the Eastern Front slows down the German offensive.
15. Kleist's and Guderian's tanks meet at Lokhvitsa, trapping four Soviet Armies. Siege of Leningrad begins.
17. *Stavka* orders the Soviet withdrawal from the Kiev area.
18–25. Battle of annihilation in Kiev pocket.
19. Germans capture Kiev.

22. Greek King George II arrives in London.
23. De Gaulle forms National Committee.
26. Hitler orders offensive against Moscow. Winter conditions halt heavy fighting east of Kiev.
28. First Arctic convoy leaves Iceland for Russia.
29. Massacre of Jews in Kiev.

October

2. Germans launch fierce attack on Moscow.
7. Panzer spearheads seal off the Vyaz'ma, Bryansk pockets. Religious freedom in Russia announced.
8. Germans take Orel.
16. Soviet Government leaves Moscow for Kuybyshev.
20. Japanese Navy prepares for Pearl Harbor attack.
21. General Zhukhov appointed commander of outer defences of Moscow.
24. Germans take Khar'kov.

29. Germans break through in Crimea.
30. Bock attacks Moscow from the north-west.

November

3. Germans capture Kursk. Yamamoto's plan to attack the U.S. fleet is approved.
9. Germans capture Yalta. Royal Navy sinks two Italian convoys.
14. The *Ark Royal* sinks while being towed to Gibraltar after a torpedo attack.
16. Germans capture Kerch'.
17. British raid German H.Q. in Libya hoping to kill Rommel.
18. Operation "Crusader": second Western Desert campaign opens.
19. British 8th Army reaches Sidi Rezegh. German raider *Kormoran* and Australian cruiser *Sydney* sink each other in battle off Australian coast.
20. Tank battle at Sidi Rezegh.
23. Rommel destroys South African 5th Brigade.
24. Auchinleck orders "Attack and pursue".
25. *Barham* sunk off Sollum.
26. Japanese carrier fleet sails. U.S. demands Japanese withdrawal from China.
27. Panzers stopped 19 miles short of Moscow.
28. Germans forced out of Rostov.

December

1. Russians counter-attack at Tula.
6. Beginning of Soviet counter-attack at Moscow.
7. Japan declares war on U.S. Pearl Harbor attacked. Japanese land in Siam and Malaya. Singapore bombed.

8. Allies declare war on Japan Russia remains neutral. Japanese begin land, sea attacks on Hong Kong, bomb Guam, Midway, Wake Island, and the Philippines.
10. Relief of Tobruk. *Prince of Wales* and *Repulse* sunk. Japanese land on Luzon.
11. Germany and Italy declare war on the U.S.
12. List replaces Bock. Royal Navy in action off Cape Bon. Withdrawal from Hong Kong mainland positions begins.
15. British withdrawal in Malaya, Burma.
17. British advance to Gazala line. Japanese land in north Borneo.
18. Japanese land on Hong Kong.
19. Italian frogmen cripple the *Queen Elizabeth* and *Valiant* in Alexandria harbour.
22. Japanese land in Lingayen Gulf. First Washington conference starts.
24. Japanese capture Wake Island.
25. British enter Benghazi. Hong Kong surrenders.

26. Japanese advance to Ipoh after break through of Perak river defences. Russian units land on Kerch' peninsula.
27. Commando raids on Germans at Vaagsö and Lofoten Islands.
29. Russians retake Kerch' and Feodosiya.
31. South Africans attack Bardia. Japanese within 30 miles of Manila.

1942

January

1. United Nations Declaration signed by 26 nations in Washington.
2. Japanese occupy Manila. Britain, U.S., U.S.S.R., China, and 22 other Allies pledge themselves not to make separate peace.
9. Russian forces enter Smolensk province.
10. A.B.D.A. Command set up under Wavell.
11. Japanese enter Kuala Lumpur.
13. Conference of Allied governments in London pledges to punish war criminals.
16. Japanese invade Burma from Siam. Heavy U.S. losses on the Bataan peninsula.
20. "Wannsee Conference" under Heydrich decides on "Final Solution of the Jewish Problem".
23. Japanese land at Rabaul, Kavieng, and Balikpapan. Russians break through between Lake Ilmen and Smolensk. Australia appeals to U.K., U.S. for reinforcements.
27. Formation of Chiefs-of-Staff Committee, Pacific Council, Anglo-U.S. Raw Materials Board.
28. Timoshenko advances into Ukraine. Rommel recaptures Benghazi.
30. British forces withdraw into Singapore, demolish causeway.

February

2. 8th Army stabilises line Gazala-Bir Hakeim.
3. Japanese begin air attacks on Port Moresby.
4. Japanese demand unconditional surrender of Singapore. Rommel captures Derna. Beaverbrook appointed Minister of Production.
5. Reinforcements arrive at Singapore.
7. Japanese land on Singapore.
8. Dr. Speer succeeds Dr. Todt.
9. Japanese take Martaban, land at Makassar.
12. *Scharnhorst, Gneisenau, Prinz Eugen* escape from Brest in "Channel Dash".